Mind You
The Realities of Mental Illness
A Compilation of Articles from the Blog Mind You

By Dr David Laing Dawson and Marvin Ross

Library and Archives Canada Cataloguing in Publication

Title: Mind you, the realities of mental illness : a compilation of articles from the blog Mind you.
Other titles: Mind you (Blog)
Names: Dawson, David Laing, 1941- author. | Ross, Marvin, 1943- author.
Description: Blog posts written by David Laing Dawson and Marvin Ross.
Identifiers: Canadiana 20189065680 | ISBN 9781927637319 (softcover)
Subjects: LCSH: Mental illness—Blogs. | LCSH: Mental health —Blogs. | LCSH: Psychiatrists—Blogs. |
LCSH: Schizophrenics—Blogs. | LCSH: Dawson, David Laing, 1941-—Blogs. | LCSH: Ross, Marvin,
1943-—Blogs. | LCGFT: Blogs.
Classification: LCC RC460 .D38 2019 | DDC 616.89—dc23

ISBN 978-1-927637-31-9 First Published by Bridgeross in Dundas, ON, Canada

Table of Contents

Introduction

We began this blog in October 2014 in order to provide commentary on the state of mental illness and its treatment for the lay public. What we provide is a viewpoint from that of a psychiatrist with many years of experience (David Laing Dawson) and a family member of someone who does have schizophrenia (Marvin Ross). Aside from his personal experience (or lived experience as it is commonly referred to), he is also a medical writer, advocate and publisher of books that take a unique look at mental illness.

To date, we have had close to 75,000 views and have been read in 151 different countries since 2014.

We also write on other topics but these are the ones on mental illness covering topics like recovery, treatments, suicide, addictions, and alternative treatments (or pseudo science).

When we began, we had this to say of our purpose:

Welcome to the launch of Mind You. While we intend to post on mental illness, mental health and life, we decided on the name **Mind You** to reflect that not everything is black and white. There are ideas and opinions but then mind you, on the other hand, one can say.......

And that is what we would like to reflect. Ideas about mental illness, health and life that can be debated and discussed so that we can come to a higher understanding of the issues. And, we have separated out mental illness from mental health because, despite their often interchangeability, they are distinct.

The National Alliance on Mental Illness defines mental illness as a medical condition that disrupts a person's thinking, feeling, mood, ability to relate to others and daily functioning. Just as diabetes is a disorder of the pancreas, mental illnesses are medical conditions that often result in a diminished capacity for coping with the ordinary demands of life. Serious mental illnesses include major depression, schizophrenia, bipolar disorder, obsessive compulsive disorder (OCD), panic disorder, post traumatic stress disorder (PTSD) and borderline personality disorder.

On the other hand, the World Health Organization defines mental health as a state of well-being in which every individual realizes his or her own potential, can cope with the normal stresses of life, can work productively and fruitfully, and is able to make a contribution to her or his community. That is quite different from mental illness.

Unfortunately there is a tendency to confuse these and organizations like the Mental Health Commission of Canada have a tendency to talk about mental health issues and problems which are not the same as mental illnesses.

Both Dr David Laing Dawson and I (Marvin Ross) will be posting on a regular basis on a variety of topics.

The posts we have selected for this volume are the most widely read over the past 4 years.

Belief Systems, Mad in America and Anti-Psychiatry

By Marvin Ross

I keep reading comments from people wondering how anyone could possibly support Donald J Trump. Fact checking his statements demonstrates how wrong he is on much of what he says. And then there are the numerous comparisons of statements that he makes that contradict each other.

Not so surprising, sadly enough, when we look at the people who believe what Robert Whitaker and the anti-psychiatry movement believe.

Put simply, Whitaker and the Mad in America anti-psychiatry folks are adamant that anti-psychotic medication for schizophrenia makes people sick and shortens their lives. Research fails to support these contentions but they persist and the data is ignored. The two latest studies provide overwhelming evidence that anti-psychotics help – but more on that in a moment.

The late Dr William M. Glazer of Yale writing in Psychiatric Times four years ago had this to say of Whitaker:

Should we accept the analysis of a journalist who (1) to my knowledge, has not treated a patient or implemented a study and (2) reaches conclusions that run counter to well-established practice guidelines? Whitaker's ideological viewpoint, which is implied throughout the book, is that our guidelines are inaccurate and driven by industry and our own need for income—that we are dishonest brokers. Beauty is in the eye of the beholder.

Criticisms of Whitaker have been done by many eminent psychiatrists but my favourite is by blogger Natasha Tracy in Healthyplace.com. Natasha explained why she refused to even read his book with these words:

Sure, he cites studies, he just contraindicates what the study actually proves. And nothing ticks me off more than this because people believe him just because there is a linked study – no one ever bothers to check that the study says whatever Whitaker *says* it does.

Except, of course, the people who do – the doctors. You know, the people who went to medical school for over a decade. You know, the people actually qualified to understand what all the fancy numbers mean. You know, those people.

And I, for one, rely a lot on what doctors make of medical data and they are the ones most able to refute Whitaker's claims.

As for the contention by Whitaker and his minions that anti-psychotics make people sick, let's look at two recent studies.

In 2013, the highly respected British Medical Journal, The Lancet, published a German meta-analysis on the efficacy and side effect profile of all anti-psychotics. The results are summarized simply in a blog by Dr Gerhard Gründer with a link to the original study.

The meta-analysis combined 212 studies with a total of 43,049 patients. All of the anti-psychotics produced improvements that were statistically better than placebo. The best agent was clozapine.

The most recent study was conducted in the Province of Quebec and published in July and was based on real world evaluations of all people prescribed with anti-psychotics for schizophrenia between January 1998 and December 2005. The cohort consisted of 18 869 patients. Outcome measures consisted of mental health event (suicide, hospitalization or emergency visit for mental disorders) and physical health event (death other than suicide, hospitalization or emergency visit for physical disorders).

The researchers pointed out that data from randomized control trials are often limited in terms of generalizability thus real world studies like this one are much more realistic. What they found was that taking anti-psychotics reduced the risk of having either a mental or a physical problem compared to those who discontinued taking them. The only anti-psychotic that performed poorly was quetiapine (seroquel) while clozapine had the best results.

The other criticism from the anti-psychiatry bunch is that taking anti-psychotics results in premature death for people with schizophrenia. Studies have shown that people with schizophrenia do die years earlier than others but the reasons are not well understood.

One hypothesis that I mention in my book *Schizophrenia Medicine's Mystery Society's Shame* is discrimination by health care practitioners. Studies show that people with schizophrenia often do not get adequate basic medical care and treatment.

Researchers in Sweden conducted a real world analysis of 21,492 patients with schizophrenia. Subjects were followed up from 2006 through 2010. Data on drug use and outcomes was obtained from national registers.

What was found was that Antipsychotics and antidepressants were associated with a **significant reduction in mortality compared with no use**. The opposite of what the anti-psychiatry crowd claim. However, there was a clear dose-response curve for benzodiazepine exposure and mortality. More benzos, greater mortality. Note that benzodiazepine drugs are not anti-psychotic medications. They provide short term relief from anxiety, but they are addictive when used over a long period. Which means with long term use people develop tolerance and then crave more. And if they stop them they experience serious withdrawal symptoms. They are never prescribed alone to treat psychosis.

Psychotropic medications prescribed properly to those who need it, are beneficial despite what you may hear from some journalists and a vocal minority.

Addendum to Belief Systems, Mad in America and Anti-psychiatry

By Dr David Laing Dawson and Marvin Ross

Reading the comments to this blog and others of ours, there is a lot of a-historic and naive thinking. Recently, someone posted my Huffington Post blog on Open Dialogue in Finland to the Spotlight on Mental Health group set up by the Boston Globe to foster discussion of their series on the sad state of mental illness treatment and care in Massachusetts. One person criticized it claiming that I had no right to comment because I have never been to Finland, and the Finnish psychiatrist I quoted had no right to be critical because he had never been to Lapland. This is part of what that person said:

"That paper by Marvin Ross is written around totally wrong information:

1) Marvin Ross has never been to Lapland to check what he wrote; thus he does not know what he speaks about...

2) The psychiatrist whom he telephoned in Helsinki, i.e. some 800 km from Lapland, had never been either...How she knew any of that I do not know."

One person commented on this blog that 10 times as many people diagnosed with schizophrenia die in the first year post diagnosis than 100 years ago and that olanzapine has killed 200,000 people worldwide.

Taking data from a number of public sources, Dr. Dawson put these statistics together:

Some American Statistics

1880

Total population: 50,000,000

A total of 91,959 "insane persons" were identified, of which 41,083 were living at home, 40,942 were in "hospitals and asylums for the insane," 9,302 were in almshouses, and only 397 were in jails. The total number of prisoners in all jails and prisons was 58,609, so that **severely mentally ill inmates constituted only 0.7 percent of the population of jails and prisons.**

Average Life expectancy for entire population: **low 40's for whites**

Low 30's for blacks

2016

2016 total population: 324,000,000

Average life expectancy: **men 76, women 81** (lower than Canada and most of Europe, lower still for minority groups. Much of this improvement from 1880 by preventing childhood diseases.)

U. S. Prison population : 2,200,000 (2014)

Or 716 per 100,000 American citizens are in prison. (a seven fold increase from 1880)

Mentally ill in prison estimated/measured to be **30% to over 50%**

So 700,000 to over one million mentally ill are incarcerated in US prisons.

Incarceration in jail reduces life expectancy by roughly a factor of **10 years for every 5 years incarcerated. (all inmates)**

Estimates/measurements of homeless in the USA: **1.5 to 2 million**.

Estimates of homeless mentally ill range from **30% to over 50%.**

So 500,000 to one million mentally ill are either homeless or living in shelters.

The homeless mentally ill are not receiving consistent psychiatric treatment. The incarcerated mentally ill may be receiving some limited treatment.

Adding this up:

One to two million mentally ill people are either homeless or incarcerated in prison in the USA.

A high proportion of people with severe mental illness live in poverty.

Severe mental illness without treatment confers higher risks and co-morbidities for several serious diseases, such as cardio vascular disease. People with severe mental illness have a much higher risk of cigarette smoking and poor diet.

Untreated depression, bipolar disorder, and schizophrenia confer a much higher risk of suicide.

Homelessness and incarceration in and of itself reduces life

expectancy by a considerable number of years. Neither of these groups is consistently receiving psychiatric treatment.

Psychiatric drugs do have side effects. (as do all pharmaceuticals) In a good outpatient or inpatient facility these can be monitored and treatment adjusted in partnership with patients.

But the real causes of contemporary poor life expectancy of the seriously mentally ill can be found in:

- **The illness itself untreated**
- **Reduction and closing of hospitals.**
- **Incarceration in jails and prisons**
- **Poor or no housing. Homelessness**
- **Poverty**
- **Poor diet. Illicit drug use. Smoking.**
- **Stigma leading to isolation and victimization**
- **Poor, inadequate, or limited health care**
- **Absence of good consistent psychiatric treatment.**

And the overall cost of not providing good early consistent psychiatric treatment in both inpatient and outpatient facilities is calculated in the following article:

http://www.usatoday.com/story/news/nation/2014/05/12/mental-health-system-crisis/7746535/

Why I've Been Prescribing Psychiatric Medication For 47+ Years

By Dr David Laing Dawson

In **1968** the police brought a very tall man to the emergency department of a large urban hospital. I quickly learned the man had two PhD's, one in literature and one in Library Sciences and he was employed as the chief librarian of an important Canadian Library. He was also manic. He could not sit still; he could not stop talking. What spewed from his mouth was a fascinating, pressured, endless run-on sentence of literary quotations, interpretations, criticisms, philosophical observations, and trivia.

The emergency department was designed as an oval, so it was possible to walk the corridor in a continuous circle of approximately 200 feet. This we did. I kept pace as he strode, talked, ranted, and raved, around and around that oval. I carried with me a glass of water and a pocket of tablets in my little white intern's jacket. Every second or third circuit when he paused briefly to catch his breath I offered him a tablet and a sip of water. He accepted this, swallowed the tablet and continued his journey. I tried to remember some of what he said. I wish I had had a tape recorder handy. His observations roamed over much of English Literature and the history of western thought, in fragments, non sequiturs, creative associations and rhyming couplets.

The tablets in my pocket each contained 100 mg of **Chlorpromazine**. At four hundred milligrams he slowed at little. By the time I had given him 600 mg he was able to pause. And finally, at perhaps 800 mg and the passage of the better part of an hour, he could sit. The pressure in his speech diminished. He could now absorb his environment. I could now speak a little and he could now hear me.

In **1970** a dishevelled, tall bearded man was brought to a hospital by his family. They had found him, after months of searching, standing outside the Vancouver library in the rain. He had been sleeping rough;

he was malnourished; he was not speaking. He was also a lawyer who had disappeared from his office practice, and his family, after announcing he was running for parliament, emptying his bank account, and then being briefly arrested for causing a disturbance. Now he was homeless, depressed, not communicating.

With clean clothes, a soft bed, good food, friendly nurses, and my anti-depressant medication, he was soon talking, more animated. But then he swung into a manic state: over-talking, grandiose, agitated, irritable, demanding. He wouldn't sit in my office. He stood, paced, demanded I let him leave, ranted invective at my profession, my interpretations of reality, refused my pills. He stood and paced. I sat and listened. He didn't leave, though the doors were never locked. His family let him know he needed to stay and accept treatment. The law society told him they would not reinstate him without treatment and a doctor's note. Eventually he sat. Eventually we talked. He accepted my pills, my mood stabilizing medication, **lithium**. Eventually he was reunited with his family. Eventually he got his licence back. He became an outpatient. He re-established his practice, stayed on his medication, and asked me if I would like to play squash with him.

In **1978** parents brought a young man to see me. He was mute. He had stopped talking altogether. I had a white board in my office, and pads and pencils. The young man was willing to sit and respond to questions by writing out his answers. I found he dare not speak because if he did some tragic event would occur in the world. People would die. He knew this because it had happened. He had become angry, and had taken the Lord's name in vain, and an earthquake had killed hundreds of people in the Middle East. He agreed to return to live with his parents, to eat and shower and sleep, and to swallow before bed each night the small tablet of **Perphenazine** I prescribed, and come to see me weekly. He came each week, and each week for an hour he wrote his answers on my white board, and when he tired of that, on the pad of paper I gave him. On his ninth visit I handed him the pad of paper. He put it aside and said, "We don't need that anymore."

On a lovely Sunday morning in June of **2008** my wife and I went for a walk. On the journey back I pondered ways to spend a leisurely afternoon. But then we found a frantic woman waiting for us in our parking lot. "John is psychotic again," she said. John is her brother. An hour later I was in their father's house. John was on the back porch smoking and pacing. I joined him there. He was agitated, mumbling half sentences in a semi-coherent fashion, some to himself, some to me. Changeable moods swept across him. His eyes would light up and he would tell himself and me that he was Jesus, and he had a mission to save the world, and that I would be forgiven, and then his mood would quickly darken, and he was evil, perhaps the devil himself, and that he should be punished, that he should destroy himself, and then just as quickly back to Jesus. I offered him a wafer of **Zydis**, a rapidly dissolving form of **Olanzapine**. He ignored this. His moods and thoughts continued to shift from Jesus to the devil, from good to evil, from a mission to save the world, to the need to destroy himself. I offered the wafer again, and this time he took it and let it dissolve in his mouth. A half hour later he was able to come into the house, and sit, and to sit quietly, and sip tea, and then to speak more rationally. Over the next few hours he became more coherent, better able to focus on the reality at hand. He would stay this night at his father's, take another Zydis before bed, and they would come and see me in the morning.

It is now **2015**. I am astonished to learn that there are people today, even some mental health professionals, who do not believe in the existence of mental illness, nor of the efficacy of psychiatric medications. I suspect that the closest brush they have had with insanity and pharmaceuticals is reading Jack Kerouac and William Burroughs in college, and the only knowledge they have of mental illness, and of the fate of the mentally ill before these medications were developed, has come from Hollywood, or the episode of Murdoch Mysteries I watched last night.

A Psychiatrist Critiques Open Dialogue

By Dr David Laing Dawson

We humans are a strange and contradictory species. While most of us are willing to take any number of potions and pills to limit the effect of the common cold, to boost our energy levels, to ward off aging, sore joints, and failing libidos, and a great many of us are willing to consume dangerous liquids, pills, and injectables to ameliorate the anxiety of knowing we are vulnerable, mortal and inconsequential life forms, and some of us decide to undergo toxic chemotherapy for a ten percent better chance of survival, there are others of us (perhaps not different people) who would deny (proven effective) antipsychotic drugs to someone suffering the devastating and dangerous symptoms of psychosis, of schizophrenia.

Even if some form of two year intensive counseling/therapy/group therapy worked as well as four weeks of Olanzapine, what on earth would be the justification for withholding the Olanzapine?

To be fair we have been here before. We have all, including psychiatrists, wanted to see, to understand, mental illness, both in mild form and severe form, as adaptations and temporary aberrations of the workings of the mind. And, by extension, amenable to persuasion, love, kindness, respect, and a healthy life style. In the Moral Treatment era of the mid to late 1800's that healthy life style was based in Christian principals of routine, work, duty, etiquette, and prayer in a pastoral setting. For someone with a psychotic illness this undoubtedly would be preferable to the imprisonment that came before, to the massive overcrowded mental hospitals that grew and grew after the industrial revolution, and even, for many, preferable to the mental health systems of 2015. But it did not treat or cure psychosis.

Through the 40's, 50's and 60's many notable psychoanalysts tried treating schizophrenia with their own particular form of "open dialogue". I read many of their books and case histories. And while they are fascinating explorations of the human condition and equally interesting attempts to find meaning within madness, it did not work, at least not as a treatment to alleviate suffering and disability.

And then in the sixties and early seventies we experimented with therapeutic communities. When I listen to the staff of Open Dialogue in Finland talking about their program I can imagine my colleagues and I saying the same things about our experience in Therapeutic Communities of the 1960's. It was humbling, as close to a level playing field as possible, a marvelous learning experience for staff, a laboratory of interpersonal and group dynamics, an open, respectful environment for patients, but it was not an effective treatment for psychotic illness, at least not without the addition of anti psychotic medication.

Harry Stack Sullivan, a psychiatrist working before the introduction of chlorpromazine wrote that "schizophrenics are not schizophrenic with me." And what he meant, I think, was that, with a little skill, plus respect, patience, a non-judgmental attitude, knowing when to talk and when to listen, knowing what to avoid and what to ignore, one can have an enlightening and pleasant conversation (dialogue) with someone suffering from Schizophrenia. But that conversation is not a lasting treatment or cure.

It is also notable, I think, that the psychiatrist and director of Open Dialogue in Finland, in interview, acknowledged that she prescribes neuroleptic medication for "about 30 percent" of their patients. Now, from what I know of human nature and our tendency to round our figures up or down depending on the social moment, maybe that is 35 to 40%. And given the way they work as a 24 hour on call mobile immediate response team, with no filters for severity or urgency, even if only 30% receive neuroleptic medication, it sounds about right. In truth then, Open Dialogue in Finland is NOT not using neuroleptic medication to treat people with severe psychotic illness.

I have no doubt that they have created relationships and a social environment for their patients in which less medication is necessary to help them survive and function. I think it is the same thing our ancestors did in the moral treatment era, and again, what we did in some therapeutic communities of the 1960's.

Open Dialogue also reminded me of some other experiments with around-the-clock, immediate response teams preventing hospitalization and achieving better results than hospitalization. When

I explored some of these in the 1970's and 1980's wondering if they could be reproduced outside of their funded clinical trials I found young idealistic doctors and nurses quite willing at that time in their lives to be on call 24/7 without extra pay, with limited personal life during the course of the experiment. We could approximate these programs in real life but we could not replicate them.

We have ample reason to not trust big pharma and their incessant push to expand their customer base, but let us also be aware of both history, and the realities that surround us, of the many people with psychotic illness now back on the streets, in the hostels and jails, of the need for better mental health care systems, and the need for better cost effective treatment, and of the many people for whom our current medications have been both sanity and life-saving.

Time to Re-evaluate Clozapine Use for Improved Schizophrenia Outcomes

By Marvin Ross

The gold standard treatment for schizophrenia has been available since the 1960s but, other than in China, it is rarely used. Given its superiority over other treatments and the improvements those on it demonstrate, it is time for governments to rethink its use. It has the potential to improve lives and to reduce the costs associated with chronic schizophrenia.

Clozapine (clozaril) was introduced in the early 1960s by the Swiss pharmaceutical company Sandoz (now Novartis) as a treatment that avoided many of the side effects of the drugs then in use. Unfortunately, it was quickly withdrawn when a rare blood disorder called agranulocytosis was discovered. This is a condition that represses the white blood cells leaving the person open to infections. The incidence of this condition is only 1-2% and it can be prevented by ensuring (as is done now) that everyone on clozapine have regular blood tests.

Because the incidence of this side effect is minimal, can be prevented before it becomes a problem with blood testing, and clozapine has shown to be superior for all symptoms of schizophrenia, it was granted a license in the US and Canada in 1990 and 1991. At the same time, a number of new anti-psychotics were introduced that were hoped to be as efficacious as clozapine but without the blood side effect.

Clozapine still shows greater efficacy than all the others. I've heard psychiatrists say that if they had a child develop schizophrenia, they would put him/her on it. But, it is reserved only for people who have treatment resistant schizophrenia and have failed to show significant improvement with 2 or 3 of the other agents. Most jurisdictions will only fund its use through a special drug program so they can monitor blood as is the case in Ontario. That makes it difficult for many doctors to enroll their patients who might benefit.

And while regular blood testing may be expensive, it is likely considerably less expensive than poor outcomes. A 2013 study of Canadians taking clozapine found that "In the pre-clozapine period more than 50% of the patients had at least 2 hospitalizations, this proportion decreased dramatically to 13% after clozapine was initiated. More than 55% of patients had no hospitalizations during clozapine therapy."

A 2012 US study summarized the benefits of clozapine as:

reducing the number of suicides;

greater reduction in the positive symptoms (delusions, voices);

improvement in cognition contributing to better work and social function; higher quality of life and longer time to discontinuation; and,

decreased relapse.

This last point, the author suggests, results in those taking it preferring it to other treatments.

The most recent study on clozapine came out this June and was conducted by scientists at the Centre for Addiction and Mental Health in Toronto. They found that the major metabolite of clozapine helps protect or enhance working memory function in people with schizophrenia. Commenting on this research, Carrie Jones of Vanderbilt University who was not involved in the work had this to say. "This study is very encouraging because the current treatments for the cognitive deficit in schizophrenia are only marginally effective. To have data that suggest a path forward for enhancing cognition by any approach is tremendously important".

Despite these positives, the use of clozapine remains underutilized in the US, UK, Canada, New Zealand and Australia. In the US, it is estimated that only 3% of patients are on clozapine. In fact, According to Herbert Y. Meltzer, MD, Professor of Psychiatry at the Vanderbilt University School of Medicine, "leading economists have cited underuse of clozapine for treatment resistance and suicide as one of the two greatest failures of mental health providers to practice evidence based medicine."

Meltzer also commented that "The fear of agranulocytosis is grossly exaggerated. The risk of its occurrence is way under one percent and the risk of death from agranulocytosis, with monitoring and treatment, is less than one percent of that." When monitored correctly, the frequency of agranulocytosis with clozapine has been estimated to be as low as 0.38 percent.

As any new and improved treatments for this horrific disease seem to be way off in the future, policy makers really should look at increasing the availability of clozapine. In China, clozapine is the most used anti-psychotic and we should catch up for the sake of those who are ill.

Disclosure – I am not funded nor am I in the pay of Novartis or any pharmaceutical companies that manufacture clozapine/clozaril.

A Psychiatrist Discusses Hearing Voices

By Dr David Laing Dawson

In the winter of 1968 I finished a 24-hour shift in the emergency department of a major Toronto Hospital, changed quickly, and walked out into the still dark morning to catch the trolley on Bathurst St. I heard my name called, over and over. I looked for the source. It seemed to come from the electrical wires strung high above the street. I got on the uptown trolley. I looked at my fellow passengers. They were each oblivious, each locked in their own private early morning thoughts within their heavy winter coats.

Sleep deprivation and stress.

I don't remember the particular stress of that 7 AM to 7 AM shift, but in 24 hours it must have included some bleeding, screaming, and dying, some vomit and rage and insanity, some crying and bewilderment, some failure.

I have no doubt that it is a simple slippage in our brains that can take our thoughts, our inner dialogue, our inner fears and our self-reassurance, and have us hear them, hear them as if either coming from outside our heads, or from an 'other' in our heads. In fact, when you think about it, it seems quite remarkable that usually our brains can make a clear distinction between the inner and the outer. So I am not surprised the boundary can be so easily broken in times of high anxiety, fear, stress, sleep-deprivation, psychosis, brain impairment, and trauma.

I am also not surprised that these voices often carry one of two kinds of meaning: accusations, fears, nasty directives or calming, reassuring, comforting messages. The phenomena that might be more difficult to understand are the hearing of conversations, undecipherable mutterings, even crowds shouting at one another. But then again, if our thoughts are often conflicted, unclear, inarticulate, there is no reason to assume thoughts that become voices would be otherwise.

In the many years since 1968 I have talked to hundreds of people who hear or have heard “voices”.

The most common of these is the hypnagogic experience, occurring in the moments between wakefulness and falling asleep, and the hypnopompic experience during the process of wakening. I’m sure we have all experienced, at times, the overlapping of dream states and wakefulness, with sounds and images from from each world colliding. As a psychiatrist though, I usually hear about it from a parent or patient worried that it is a harbinger of something serious. It is not. Though this overlap can be increased by drugs that alter the rhythms of sleep, and by anxiety and stress and sleep deprivation.

Then we have the shy, anxious, overly-selfconscious teenagers who imagine, and then feel, and then think they hear their peers speak about them in the crowded hallways and cafeterias of school. For the boys it is usually an accusation of failure, of stupidity, of weakness, of failed or unwelcome sexuality. For the girls it can have more to do with dress, complexion, blemishes, size, being alien, as well as stupid, a loser. If it is the product of anxiety, social anxiety, in this age group, the teen usually, once away from the experience, understands he or she probably imagined it.

But it is often the reason they refuse to go to school, isolate themselves, become depressed. It is painful for them. And it is alleviated by good counsel and medication.

(Of course there are also instances of groups of teenagers actually systematically taunting and commenting on a schoolmate’s shortcomings)

The next most common cause of hallucinations may be brain impairment, from injury, disease, toxic substances, withdrawal from alcohol, or dementia. And these experiences of imaginary people, imaginary events, fearful reactions, and conversations with visual and auditory hallucinations are scattered, disjointed, intermittent, chaotic, changeable. They also may overwhelm reality, replace it. And if the brain impairment can be treated they go away.

And then the psychotic illnesses: In the exalted state of mania with its feelings of power, of influence, of supreme importance (often accompanied by sleep deprivation), the thought that becomes a voice often belongs, as one might anticipate, to God. And the messages are prophetic and instructive. Usually instructions to share one's new found wisdom. But sometimes they draw on the Old Testament and include fire, flood, pestilence and vengeful punishment.

Fortunately we now have medicines that quell acute mania in short order, and prevent, if taken regularly, relapses.

In the past it was not uncommon for a manic person to die of exhaustion, pneumonia, exposure, or to wreak some havoc, before coming back to earthbound reality.

And then we have a psychotic depression. Again if the boundary between thought and auditory experience is broken, the thought-voices align with the person's mood. They are dark, hopeless, foreboding. They speak of death and disease. Usually the sufferer's death and disease, but sometimes, with some men and women, the death of their family as well.

Undiagnosed and untreated a psychotic depression often leads to tragedy. Again, fortunately, our modern treatments, including ECT, are very effective.

And then we have the schizophrenias. In my experience the hearing of voices is just one part of schizophrenia, a small part, though often very distressing to the sufferer. Many don't admit to voices until years later. (For over a year it had remained a puzzle why one young man jumped off a school roof. Until he was well enough and he trusted me enough to tell me about the instructions he was receiving at the time.)

And the voices, the transformation of thoughts to an auditory experience, again follow the pattern of the sufferer's feelings, ideas, distorted interpretations. They are often accusatory in nature, exacerbating guilt and self-loathing. They are sometimes instructive. That is, they might propose an action that will stop the pain and suffering of others. Such as jumping off a roof.

For most people with schizophrenia who do suffer auditory hallucinations the voices are tormenting. They would like them gone. A few get used to them, learn to ignore them. A very few, eventually, allow them to become a comforting background buzz within their otherwise socially isolated lives.

And an equally common symptom of schizophrenia is the reverse: the discomforting conviction that others in your proximity can hear every thought you have. Your thoughts are being broadcast as it were.

(The treatment of schizophrenia is addressed in many other blogs on this site.)

Trauma. Abuse. It is again not really surprising that during acute trauma, during the experience of pain, fear and the threat of death and of absolute powerlessness to change this, our brains can take us elsewhere, that they have mechanisms at hand in these dire circumstances to transport us to kinder experiences in our imagination. For a child this may include being a different child with reassuring caregivers, better parents, a much more benevolent world. The more prolonged the abuse the more complex and real the imagined world may become. It could include multiple thought/voices that reassure and comfort. And others that threaten and punish.

The adult who survives this may carry with him or her both a hypersensitivity to threat, to the faces, noises, smells and symbols of threat, quick and exaggerated fear reactions, as well as an ability to call up, to return to, to run to, the other worlds of reassurance and comfort.

This is not schizophrenia. It is PTSD. We don't have pills that fix this. Though we do have some that may improve sleep, alleviate some anxiety, and quell the most extreme reactions. And to focus on strength, to find a way to deny the memories, thoughts and voices that threaten, punish, and degrade, and to lean on the thoughts and voices that support, comfort and empower, is a good and courageous survival mechanism.

If the voice is comforting and supporting, and not interfering with one's ability to live and survive and function in our tangible world, I would not want to try to quell it.

Is There a Professional Turf War in the Mental Health Field?

By Marvin Ross – First published in the Huffington Post on March 9, 2015

One of my pet peeves is the use of the term "mental health problems and issues" to reflect mental illness. Some have told me that if we imply that people are mentally ill then we are stigmatizing them because we are saying that there is something wrong with their brain. Well, there is, and so what? With cancer, we don't say someone has cell problems and issues but rather they have cancer and we are usually pretty specific because there are so many different forms of cancer each with its own unique outcomes.

And the same goes for mental illness. But, someone recently pointed out to me that the reason we use the vague term "mental health problems and issues" is that what we are seeing is a turf war amongst professionals. And I think that person is right.

When we think of an illness, we think medical doctor. When you are ill, you see an MD who uses diagnostic skills, tests, imaging — a methodology developed over time, to determine what the problem is. Once determined, the MD decides on a course of action (with the patient) which may include referral to another more appropriate health professional (dietitian, counsellor, medical specialist, hospitalization) or medication. The MD is at the apex of the pyramid and the gatekeeper for others.

Now as my cynical friend stated, there is only one relatively finite pot of money for services for the mentally ill and, if we call it an illness, then the medical docs are going to get most of it. Other professionals will get the crumbs. However, if we don't call it an illness but a problem, then it becomes more appropriate for other professionals like psychologists, social workers and others to be the first line of assessment and treatment.

Last year, one of my blogs upset the Canadian Psychological Association because I pointed out that in 2006, they were concerned that the newly formed Mental Health Commission of Canada would focus on mental illness to the exclusion of mental disorders and behavioural health. That generated a reply from Karen Cohen, the CEO of the CPA.

In November of last year, the British Psychological Society issued a report called Understanding Psychosis and Schizophrenia where they conclude that "psychosis can be understood and treated in the same way as other psychological problems such as anxiety or shyness." And that "Hearing voices or feeling paranoid are common experiences which can often be a reaction to trauma, abuse or deprivation. Calling them symptoms of mental illness, psychosis or schizophrenia is only one way of thinking about them, with advantages and disadvantages." And they conclude that "Psychological therapies — talking treatments such as Cognitive Behaviour Therapy (CBT) — are very helpful for many people."

What they have done is to trivialize schizophrenia and suggest that its treatment be shifted to themselves and that they can uncover the underlying trauma that is the cause over the course of many talk sessions and help.

To be fair, before they had any effective treatments, psychiatrists tried this as well, and it did not work.

First out of the gate to criticize this report were three bloggers on theMental Elf. Keith Laws, a Professor of Cognitive Neuropsychology, analyzed their claim on the efficacy of CBT and found that the research does not support the statement that it is as effective a treatment as medication. Alex Langford, a psychiatry trainee who also studied psychology, challenged their conclusions on medication and pointed out that there is "solid evidence for elevated presynaptic dopamine levels being a key abnormality in psychosis, and there is copious evidence that inhibiting the action of this excess dopamine using antipsychotics leads to clinical improvement in psychosis." Samei Huda, a Consultant Psychiatrist, points out that the "reduction of psychosis to just hallucinations and delusions is flawed." He points out that "Cognitive impairment and negative symptoms (depression, lack of enjoyment, lethargy) are important as they often have a bigger effect on social functioning than hallucinations or delusions."

James Coyne, a psychologist himself and one who is very critical of his colleagues, pointed out that:

Key stakeholders were simply excluded — primary care physicians, social workers, psychiatrists, police and corrections personnel who must make decisions about how to deal with disturbed behavior, and — most importantly — the family members of persons with severe disturbance. There was no check on the psychologists simply slanting the document to conform to their own narrow professional self-interests, which we are asked to accept as 'expertise'.

He goes on to say that this paper is not evidence based and that "quotes are carefully selected to support the psychologists opinions expressed before the document was prepared — like 15 years ago in their Recent Advances in Understanding Mental Illness and Psychotic Experiences. "

Dr Ronald Pies, a psychiatrist, writes that what is missing from the report "is any deep understanding of the psychic suffering occasioned by severe and enduring psychotic states, including but not limited to schizophrenia." The psychologists see psychosis and schizophrenia simply as hearing voices that others do not and/or having fears or beliefs that those around us do not share. Pies points out that this is a shallow and superficial description of the psychotic experience and does scant justice to the nightmarish reality of severe psychotic states.

In fact, he finds that the psychologists responsible for this report do nothing but trivialize the profound suffering that is psychosis and schizophrenia.

It is well to remember that the prime directive for any physician, including psychiatrists, is not to "be clever"; not to "define abnormal," not even "to diagnose," but to reduce suffering.

And while the psychologists lobby for a greater piece of the treatment pie or, as Coyne says slanting to there own "narrow professional self-interests," and debate with other professionals, the suffering of those with the most serious of mental health problems and issues — real illnesses — continues.

Families of the Seriously Mentally Ill Need Support Too

By Marvin Ross

It is said that it takes a village to raise a child. But, if that child grows up and develops a serious mental illness, the village often disappears and the parents are left on their own. One of the most poignant descriptions of community response to a parent with a mentally ill child versus a child with another type of illness was provided by Laura Pogliano, a mother and advocate in Maryland. It is a very long list but the bottom line is:

"Your child is not homeless. Your child is not incarcerated for years. Your child is not maligned in general by society. Your child's illness is not romanticized or mythologized with ideas like "Madness is Genius." Your child is not part of the Gun Control debate. Your child is not automatically part of the legal system. Your child does not have a Preventable Tragedies national database. Your child is not a throwaway. Mine is all of these things."

And the stress of both having a child with a serious mental illness and the lack of empathy from many can be overwhelming. The European Federation of Families of People with Mental Illness (EUFAMI), a European non-profit organization that primarily advocates on behalf of families and family carers, has just released the results of a survey they conducted on the impact of serious mental illness on families.

The results are not pretty!

The survey of 400 people so far was conducted in Australia, Canada, France, Germany, Italy, Spain and the UK and was designed to understand the needs and challenges of those caring for relatives with severe mental illness, in particular schizophrenia. It will continue collecting data till the end of this year.

Almost half the participants (46%) were not happy with the support they've received from medical/healthcare staff and 38% do not believe they are taken seriously. 44% are not satisfied with their ability to influence decisions about the care of their relatives.

Four out of 10 of the family caregivers feel they cannot cope while 1 in 3 suffer depression, 1 in 3 worry about their own physical health as a result of their burden and 1 in 3 are close to the breaking point. Almost all (90%) want and need help with their burden.

Caring for a family member, the survey concluded, was similar to having a part time job involving an additional 23 hours a week and a job that often lasts for the rest of their lives. As Kevin Jones, the Secretary General of EUFAMI said, "this hidden workforce of family carers is a lifeline for society and we must take steps to ensure they are fully recognised for their contributions, their voices are heard and they are supported in order to allow them to continue caring effectively and safely for their loved ones, without putting their own physical and emotional well-being at risk"

Kathy Mochnacki, a mother in Richmond Hill, ON in a letter to the Toronto Star, pointed out that

"since the deinstitutionalization of hospital mental health services, family caregivers of people with serious mental illness have shouldered most of the responsibility of care and have become the default mental health system. Furthermore, we often do our work in isolation, coping with discrimination and unrealistic privacy legislation that could potentially put us and our ill relative in harm's way."

And it is that absurd privacy legislation that is a large source of the stress felt be caregivers. Imagine having an adult child with life threatening cancer and being told by the medical profession that they cannot talk to you because of privacy. A sick child of any age needs all the help and support that they can get and it is the family who are often most in tune with their state of health. To continue to deny families information, involvement, and to refuse to listen to their suggestions is unproductive and absurd. And yet, despite recommendations to end this situation in both Canada and the US, it continues.

The Decline of Mental Illness Treatment from the 1980s On

By Dr David Laing Dawson

Through the 1970's into the 1980's I ran what we called Community Psychiatry Services. They were General Hospital based and consisted of teams of psychiatrists, nurses, social workers and psychologists. We used what we called an "Active Intake" process that ensured that the severely ill received appointments very quickly and the worried well were rerouted to other agencies. The "active" part of the intake process was a pre-appointment engagement of the patient, the family, the other caregivers. Doing this required that the clinic not become specialized, and that it did not have exclusionary criteria.

The second component necessary for this is a true team, with each member involved, the care plan decided by the team led by a psychiatrist, and that the nurses and social workers be willing to function as case managers. It also required that each member of the team be prepared to help with medication compliance and monitoring, medical care, budgeting, finding bus passes, talking to families, giving shopping lessons, helping with all activities of daily living and also counseling.

Doing this work requires a high tolerance for chaos, uncertainty, anxiety, and insanity.

What happened?

Several things I think, though it is difficult to see the forces of change while living within them.

1. The length of stay in hospitals for the mentally ill became shorter and shorter, driven at least in part by spurious management and budget ideals.

2. The mental hospitals continued to downsize, in some part as a naive ideal, but mostly as a means of shifting cost (and responsibility) from Province and State to Community and Federal Governments.

(Note the stats of the Chicago area show an exact mirror image between the declining numbers in hospitals, and the inclining numbers in jails and prisons from 1970 to 2010)

3. The general Community Psychiatry Service is not a good academic career choice. Academics need to specialize for teaching and research opportunities. Hence the development of Anxiety Disorder and Bipolar Clinics. This doesn't work for the severely mentally ill because to satisfy all the research and protocol needs the waiting list is long, the assessment phase onerous.

4. Again, based on naive idealism, many community services shifted location from the hospital to the community. But once a clinic is moved away from the hospital (geographically and managerially) several things happen:

a. They can no longer risk taking disorganized, chaotic and potentially dangerous patients and

b. Non-medical and non-psychiatric philosophies start to dominate, and the severely ill are excluded. And

c. (at least in my experience) away from the stable budget and managerial practices of a hospital, strange things happen, all the way from pop psychology to fraud.

5. I suppose it was inevitable that each discipline develop more of a sense of autonomy and independence. Social workers and other mental health professionals are no longer case managers working with psychiatrists. They are independent counselors. The development of simplistic models of counseling (CBT and DBT) which can be applied once per week for ten weeks helped this along. This has also contributed to something of an anti-pharmaceutical attitude. (By the way, there is no evidence that CBT is any more helpful than any other professional counseling relationship, but being a rigid simplistic set of responses it is easier to study)

6. I am also convinced that by putting addictions and mental health (illness) under the same umbrella, we diluted what sympathy and empathy the community was developing for the seriously mentally ill.

7. This was compounded by the so-called recovery model, which at its heart, really means (and this may be appropriate for addicts) that if you really try hard enough and think only good thoughts (CBT), and are sufficiently "supported", you can get well and recover fully.

8. The corollary of this being that if a person with a psychotic illness is not recovering it just means he is not trying hard enough.

9. De-stigmatization. I just happened to watch "Big" the other night and noticed that the actor who played a walk through part, non speaking, looking homeless and mumbling to himself in downtown New York, was listed in the credits as playing "Schizo". The real way to de-stigmatize any illness is not by feel good infomercials, but by providing adequate and successful treatment. Think Leprosy, AIDS, cancer.

10. Without a team to work with, to case manage, to field crisis calls, to make home visits, to check on progress more frequently, a lone psychiatrist will find it difficult to treat the severely ill.

11. The tightening of the mental health acts and processes in each state and province, the protection of individual rights and the provision of due process (as defined by lawyers), again based on a sort of naive idealism, resulted in four unintended consequences: thousands of people suffering from untreated psychotic illnesses in the streets and shelters, a burgeoning population of mentally ill in the prisons, the dramatic growth of locked Forensic Psychiatry Units, and a sad return to locked doors for the rest of the hospital now dominated by the Forensic units.

Between 1900 and 1960 the severely mentally ill were mostly institutionalized, treated in mental hospitals for long lengths of stay, by doctors who were often imported and/or had limited licenses. Then as now, the Academic and North American trained psychiatrists worked in private offices treating a small number of patients over many years. These patients could be counted on to be articulate, educated, and at least middle class.

Between about 1960 and 1990, with new effective medications and the move to de-institutionalize, community clinics like the ones I worked in developed in many parts of North America; the General Hospitals developed psychiatric programs, and for at least two decades, perhaps three, we seemed to be moving in the right direction. In parts of Canada incentives were developed to keep psychiatrists working in hospitals with the severely ill or as they were called then, the seriously and persistently ill. And the University Departments of Psychiatry finally took an interest in the medical treatment of the severely mentally ill.

We were going in the right direction.

And now it seems we must re-invent the wheel.

For more information on schizophrenia, check out the documentary Schizophrenia in Focus

Psychiatric Staff Burnout?

By Marvin Ross

Recently, I reviewed a book manuscript from a woman who had developed bipolar disorder in her 40s and had been hospitalized a number of times. What I found particularly interesting was that the woman had originally been trained as a nurse although she was not working in that capacity. She said that as a student nurse, she and her fellow students hated their rotation on the psychiatric ward. She admitted that she and the other students had disdain for the patients and that they felt that their illness was their own fault.

I don't know how many of those student nurses ended up working with the mentally ill nor do I know if those attitudes are held by the majority who work in this area. And, while I recognize that there are many kind and compassionate people working with the mentally ill, I've found from personal experience and from what others have told me that there are still far too many who display the same attitudes as those student nurses. Is it the attitudes they came into the field with or is it burnout? I don't know. These are but some examples reflecting attitudes between those who do work with the mentally ill and those professionals who only come in contact with them periodically.

A young man with schizophrenia had been going to a very nice community dentist who left his practice and so he asked his psychiatric case worker to recommend one. He was sent to a dentist who looked after many of the clients of this particular agency and the dentist was rude, impolite and suggested that this individual needed to have a number of teeth extracted. He complained to his caseworker and was told that many clients complained about this dentist but they had no one else they could recommend.

I referred the individual to another community dentist who saw no need to extract any teeth, was aware that his new patient had schizophrenia and bent over backwards to provide caring and compassionate service.

Now because this person is on clozapine, it requires regular blood monitoring to ensure that the white blood cells are not being depleted

– a serious side effect of this particular anti-psychotic. The agency has all its clients go to one blood lab which is not convenient for many of them who do not live near the lab. The agency refused to allow any client to have their blood taken at other labs and argued that only this particular lab could do the job as they specialized in clozapine blood work.

That was absurd as the blood work is for a white blood cell count which is a common and standard test. In fact, the blood labs that take the samples do not do the analysis as the samples are sent to a central laboratory. The real issue was that the staff of the psychiatric agency could not be bothered to write up a separate requisition for each client who wanted to go to a more convenient lab. I suspect that they had one requisition and just sent in a long list of names of clients who required the test.

When this individual went to another case management agency, the staff expressed surprise that he was only allowed to go to one inconvenient blood lab and gave him a requisition that he took to a lab withing a short walk of his home.

And, outside of the psychiatric hospital pharmacy, only one drug store dispensed clozapine so clients from that agency had to have all their prescriptions dispensed by that one pharmacy. And the staff at that pharmacy were completely rude to their customers which I observed on a number of occasions myself. Again, the new agency arranged to have the clozapine dispensed by the hospital pharmacy so the individual could take his other prescriptions to a more convenient community pharmacy. He was quite tense about the move and tremendously relieved to find that the new pharmacy was efficient and treated him with respect.

A number of years ago, I did a short piece called a Tale of Two Systems where I compared the care given to a man with schizophrenia between a specialized psychiatric group home and a residence for seniors. The relatives could not believe how much better care and respect the man received from a seniors home than he got from the psychiatric facility. In fact, the mental health staff ignored what were obvious signs of developing Parkinson's until the poor man broke his hip, developed pneumonia and ended up in a seniors home. And the relatives got much more information from the staff. They did not hide behind privacy as an excuse to ignore the family as often happens in psychiatric facilities.

Katherine Flannery Dering describes a similar situation in her book *Shot in the Head A Sister's Memoir, A Brother's Struggle* about her late brother Paul. Hospital staff in the psychiatric stream noted and ignored a tumour on Paul's lung. It was only when the family moved him into a seniors residence that the doctor also noted the existence of the tumour on his lung, had it biopsied and discovered lung cancer.

People with schizophrenia have a life expectancy that is about 20% less than others. Part of this stems from the condition itself but studies have also shown that assessment and treatment of common physical health problems in people with schizophrenia falls well below acceptable standards.

Now, I realize that It is not easy dealing with people who can be difficult and frustrating to work with because of the very nature of their illnesses. I get that but management should be better attuned to burnout if these attitudes stem from that and should develop strategies to deal with it.

I'd love to hear from others if what I've observed is as common as I've noticed and some ideas that might help burned out staff to deal with their problems.

On Solutions to Psychiatric Burnout

By Dr David Laing Dawson

The anorexic girl is down to 84 pounds. It is time for her weigh-in. She stands on the scales, dressed as before, and, lo and behold, she now weighs 84.5 pounds. Excellent. You offer praise before you notice the suspicious bulges in the pockets of her sweats. And was that a whiff of ketones you smelled on her breath?

The call comes at 11 pm. Your patient is in emergency, suicidal. How can that be? You just saw her in the afternoon and not only did she say she was doing fine, but that you had been a big help.

He is agitated today, restless; his eyes scan suspiciously. You ask about his medication and he tells you he tossed his pills in the toilet. You ask why. He tells you he doesn't need them anymore. In fact, he's never felt better. And now he knows it is true. He does have a mission to spread the word of God. Or maybe he's evil and should be killed. And then he's standing, glaring at you, and you glance at the clock and see that your next patient has probably arrived, and you haven't finished your notes from this morning, and the man in front of you was doing so well last month, and now — do you have time to talk him into going back on his meds? Is it safe to let him leave? What are the odds of the inpatient unit having a bed? What is that new process for admitting someone? And then the receptionist calls to tell you your next two patients are waiting.

He is depressed. There is no doubt he suffers from depression. Your pills, the combination he is on now, keep him functioning marginally. But he wants more Lorazepam to get through the day, and he's already taking too many. He is overweight. You've talked about diet and exercise but the chances of him following a healthy diet and exercising daily are nil. He just wants to feel better. And you would love to be able to make him feel better but... And now he's telling you he can't make it through the day without more Lorazepam and you just finished reading how this drug shortens life expectancy....

He has chronic pain. It is real, and so are his traumas. But you know there is little you can do for him but listen to his complaints about all the doctors he's seen, the insurance company, the Workers Comp, all their stupid decisions, and now because he has a tenant in his house paying rent they want to reduce his pension....So you listen, and you hope he doesn't come back to see you, but you know he will because you listen, and he survives another month, and he is a hard man to like, but ....

Ah, the weight and burden of responsibility. People talk of Compassion burnout. Listening to all those difficult lives and tragic stories day after day, and trying not to take them home with you. But the faster route to burnout that I see among mental health workers is an assumption of responsibility for events over which they have no control, leading to a sense of failure, and then cynicism, anger and blame.

In other branches of medicine and nursing, responsibilities are usually clearer, not always, but usually. Yours and your patient's responsibilities.

Perhaps you advised against flying in the third trimester, after that little bleed. But your patient ignored this advice and flew to an American city and went into premature labour. You gave her the correct advice; she is responsible for her decision to fly.

You put a cast on and advise no weight bearing for two weeks. You are fully confident your advice will be followed.

You prescribe antibiotics for bronchitis. You know she will take them as directed on the bottle. She, your patient, may even know a little about the history of antibiotics, and how they work, and accept though the drug might have side effects, the benefits outweigh the risks, and she knows as you know that when it comes to bacterial infections, Amoxicillin will work better than megavitamins and positive thinking.

He has chest pain. You ask him to take his shirt off. He complies. He lets you take his blood pressure, listen to his heart. He will wait for the ambulance, let you take a blood sample. He will let you perform an ECG, send him down for an X-ray or CT scan. When you tell him what you think his diagnosis is, he won't argue. You offer nitroglycerine and morphine. You admit him to hospital and discuss a bypass operation. He doesn't tell you he disagrees with western medicine and would rather have an incantation, a healing ceremony, or take those little brown Chinese Medicine pills.

Burn out. The problem stems from the burden of responsibility without power or control. A mental health worker who repeatedly assumes (emotionally) responsibility for that which is either not within his or her control, or only marginally so, will become stressed, cranky, dispassionate, and begin to blame the patients.

In this work, dealing with, as examples, that first grouping of anecdotes, the mental health worker must constantly monitor his or her own assumptions of responsibility, know when to act, what he can change and what he can't, when and how to assume responsibility, and when to sit back, offer compassion and understanding, but allow the universe to unfold, allow people to lead their own lives in their own way. It is a very difficult balance to maintain throughout every day of any mental health professional's life.

That first girl. She's cheating by putting rocks in her pockets, isn't she? She's making you look stupid. And you are doing your best. And it makes no sense. She is killing herself and you just can't get through to her.

If that chest pain patient in the last medical anecdote dies of cardiac arrest you will know that you did everything you could to prevent that outcome. But the suicidal patient in the emergency room? What should you do? How much can you do? Is it even feasible to try to assume some responsibility for her actions, her behaviour? Did you miss something she didn't tell you during that last visit? This is the third time she's been taken to the Emergency in as many months. You know your colleagues in that department are now blaming you. They are also wondering how come you let your psychotic patients go off their medication?

To prevent burn-out, to prevent the development of cynical attitudes, mental health workers need a supervisory support structure that understands this perennial problem, this complex burden of responsibilities, and which provides mechanisms that help deal with it, help with it. Counseling, workshops, direct help, sharing, consultation, debriefings.

And all too often that administrative and supervisory structure does the opposite. It directly or tacitly blames the mental health worker for events he or she never did have the power to control.

Naming

By Dr. David Laing Dawson

Disease, illness, affliction, problem, atypical neurological development, eccentricity, issue, alternate reality, way of life, gift? There is no shortage of words and phrases to name and describe the nature of our struggles to cope, to live and survive in our social world. But each word conveys implications of value, worth, status, promise, expectation, and responsibility. Often these implications themselves determine which word is chosen. About once a month I am told I am about to see (in consultation) a child who has been labeled "gifted". Whereupon I must try to find a delicate way of asking if "gifted" means Carnegie Hall by the age of 13, or brilliant at quantum mechanics but can't relate to people, or simply learning disordered, or, careful with these words now, mentally handicapped.

Unfortunately many of the words we use, benign and descriptive at first, over time accrue negative value like small crusty accretions. There wasn't anything wrong with "retarded" (slowed, behind) until it became an epithet in the schoolyard.

To prevent misunderstanding, but inevitably to obscure, we often fall back on what an editor friend of mine calls "weasel words", benign enough to not offend, but careless and unhelpful. "Issue" is one of those words, as in "addiction issues", and "mental health issues." I don't know why anyone would say, "He has addiction issues." rather than, "He is addicted to heroin." But they do. The use of "mental health issue" is easier to understand, though equally unhelpful. The speaker or journalist is trying to avoid the word "illness", as in "He suffers from a mental illness."

A Monty Python skit comes to mind, in which the doctor hesitates while telling his patient that he has, or suffers from, Syphilis. He gets to the word and, instead of speaking it, bends and whispers it into the open drawer of his desk. The patient doesn't hear the word and asks the doctor to say again. In Monty Python fashion this repeats over and over until....

Actually I don't remember the ending and I cannot find it on

Youtube. But I imagine Michael Palin finally screaming the word, and a few others, at John Cleese.

We avoid the word because of the stigma attached to it, thus increasing the stigma. It was not until we openly used the word "cancer", that we didn't run from it, euphemize it, hide it, that it began to lose its stigma. Once free of its stigma the doors opened, research money poured in; clinics, wards, whole hospitals were devoted to helping those who suffer from cancer. The illness cancer, the disease cancer. Not the "cancer issue".

Terry Fox did not run across Canada with a leg amputated to raise money and awareness for Bone Health Issues.

When Will All Mental Health Professionals Learn to Respect Families?

By Marvin Ross

Families of the mentally ill are the tireless workers who provide support and advocacy for their ill relatives at tremendous financial, emotional and physical costs. The families also are the ones who push for reforms from reluctant elected officials. It was families in the US who formed the National Alliance on Mental Illness (NAMI) to fight for their kids. In Canada, it was the late Bill Jeffries, a family member in Oakville, Ontario, who formed what was originally the Friends of Schizophrenics in Canada (now the Schizophrenia Society).

A group of family members in the US (partly tongue in cheek) call themselves the Sisters of Perpetual Determination to indicate their resolve.

Families fight for their ill relatives whatever the illness they suffer is – cancer, CP, autism, schizophrenia – and that is as it should be. But when it comes to mental illness, we are often not consulted and are shunned and talked down to by professionals. Just recently, a group of very dedicated families had to fight for months to have a representative on an Ontario Government Committee set up to evaluate mental health services before a family member was appointed.

But do not consider the Family Outreach and Support Program (FOR) in the same class as these aforementioned family advocacy groups. FOR which is funded in part by tax money is being integrated into the Canadian Mental Health Association Toronto Chapter. Despite the name FOR, from the writing of its founding executive director who stepped aside in 2015 but is still on staff, this group is not family friendly in my opinion.

Karyn Baker says that she is a mother of a child with mental illness but in her article entitled Families: A Help or Hindrance in Recovery she reveals what I consider to be disdain for families. I'm not sure if she still believes what she wrote as the article is no longer online but it was discussed by Susan Inman in a Huffington Post article and I do have a copy.

The article is a chapter in a book called Alternatives Beyond Psychiatry edited by a founding member of an organization called INTAR or the International Network Toward Alternatives and Recovery of which Ms Baker is or was a member (she lists her membership on her CV). The organization believes that emotional distress is often labelled as psychosis.

Here is what Ms Baker writes:

- "traditionally many families have not been given the information or strategies for helping their families in the recovery process. As a result, **families have tended to unwittingly be a hindrance** in their relative's recovery"
- "There was little, if any, mention of recovery and no critical examination of the mental health system from a trauma-informed and anti-oppression perspective. These programs created like-minded thinking between families and mental health professionals, which further reinforced the **limiting idea that mental illness is a disease and must be treated with medication or otherwise, recovery is not possible."**
- "In North America, the alliance of mental health professionals and family organizations has **entrenched the medical model of mental health distress** and has led to a**n extreme over-reliance on psychiatric medications and coercive mental health legislation.** A collateral damaging consequence has been the divisiveness between the psychiatric survivor organizations and family groups. Psychiatric survivors have been highly skeptical of family involvement in the recovery movement. **Often survivors have felt both the controlling and paternalistic (and often traumatizing) experience of both their own families as well as those of large family advocacy organizations."**
- "The ***key messages*** that families report taking away from the course are that: **recovery is possible even without any professional intervention** (for many families this is the first time they have heard this message); hope is the cornerstone to recovery – it is almost impossible to recover without hope and the family's role is to "hold the

hope"; to avoid creating learned helplessness by being overly-involved; to support risk-taking and giving the relative the dignity and freedom to fail like any other human being; to let go of controlling relative's choices – this is their recovery journey; to stop viewing everything from a problem orientation and start building on strengths; **to view madness as a human experience; don't use coercion or forced treatment; explore** alternatives and use advanced directives.

- Families also have reflected back on the importance of the group process in learning about recovery and their own behavior. **Families want a place that does not perpetuate their guilt or shame about their own role in wounding their relative but helps them to acknowledge their role and behavior and help them to make change in a safe environment.** Many families acknowledge that they started this journey as either uninformed or misinformed and that often their natural intuition as to how to be helpful was actually counter-productive. Families also become aware of their own internalized discrimination or mentalism about people with mental health issues. Families learn to use language that does not hurt or hinder recovery."

None of this is evidence based nor is it family friendly unless families admit that they have been controlling and paternalistic towards their ill loved ones. Point two from her paper is still the raison d'etre of the agency as it is prominently displayed on their website. An excellent critique of the absurdity of their "trauma-informed and anti-oppression perspective" compared to the medical model was recently provided in an excellent article in Clinical Psychiatry News entitled Unmasking Trauma-Informed Care. It makes for good reading.

And my tax dollars go to programs like this when the money could be used to provide more psychiatric beds that are desperately needed.

The Best Treatment for Psychotic Illness is no Secret.

By Dr David Laing Dawson

Nor does it require argument and more research comparing one component to another. This is it:

- Early intervention, thorough assessment.
- Treatment with medication by a knowledgeable physician/psychiatrist.
- A good working relationship between psychiatrist and patient and his or her family.
- Adequate housing with support.
- A supportive family.
- Ongoing education for patient and family about illness and treatment.
- A wise, grounded counselor/therapist/support worker.
- Easy access and rapid response support team for crises and emergencies.
- Healthy diet and exercise.
- Good general medical care.
- Membership, belonging to a group or organization of some kind.
- Daily routine.
- An activity that provides some sense of worth and value.

When the support systems are in place, and a good working relationship has developed between the psychiatrist and patient and family, pharmacological treatment can be (safely) titrated down (or up) to the lowest effective maintenance dosages. Occasionally, with close monitoring over a long period of time, this can mean trials of no medication.

In the real world there are dozens of reasons this ideal is not often achieved, or only partially achieved. And some of those reasons include the interminable nonsense spouted by the Mad in America Group, inter-professional rivalries for prestige and money, illness deniers, would-be gurus, and politicians and planners listening to this nonsense.

The Unintended Consequences of Focusing on Recovery in Schizophrenia

By Marvin Ross

Much has been said in this blog by my colleague Dr David Laing Dawson and myself on the concept of recovery. Wouldn't it be wonderful if full recovery was possible but it isn't. However, I really should clarify that somewhat. Schizophrenia should probably be referred to as a spectrum disorder like autism.

When Bleuler first coined the term in 1908, he referred to it as the schizophrenias and said that it was a physical disease process characterized by exacerbations and remissions. No one was ever completely "cured" of schizophrenia — there was always some sort of lasting cognitive weakness or defect that was manifest in behavior. Unfortunately, over the years, it began to be considered to be one disease only.

In a recent article in Psychology Today, University of Toronto medical historian, Edward Shorter, had this to say. In adolescent-onset schizophrenia, some don't recover at all; others make only a "social recovery," and some maybe go on to have a normal life or "Maybe not". Shorter then adds that "The field has made virtually no progress in unpacking chronic severe illness and differentiating out several distinct entities. In no other field of medicine would this be conceivable!" and "Some involve loss of brain tissue, others don't. Some have to stay on meds, others don't. Some get well, others don't. These are not all the same illness!"

In fact, it has long been recognized that there are three outcomes to schizophrenia. Roughly a third are treatment resistant and remain very ill, a third can be helped with meds and other treatment modalities to improve sufficiently to lead a reasonable but disabled life, and a third will have one psychotic episode, receive treatment and never have another or any long term deficits.

According to the Treatment Advocacy Center, 10 years after diagnosis, "one-fourth of those with schizophrenia have recovered completely, one-fourth have improved considerably, and one-fourth have improved modestly. Fifteen percent have not improved, and 10 percent are dead."

How do you think the families of the majority of those with non recoverable schizophrenia or the individuals themselves will feel when we hold up to them what is achievable by only 25%? And, we tell them that it is achievable. Why can't I (or my son or daughter) achieve that. Have I done something wrong? Cancer is an interesting analogy. There is not one cancer but many. And each cancer has its own unique characteristics and prognosis.

Non melanoma skin cancer (basal cell and squamous cell) have 5 year survivals of 95% and 90%. In contrast, the 5 year survival for pancreatic cancer ranges from 1% for stage IV to 14% from stage 1A. Imagine if we told those with stage IV pancreatic cancer not to worry because 5 year survival is 95%. Ridiculous isn't it but that is what we tell people with schizophrenia. Don't worry, you should be able to recover because 25% do.

Now, I'm not saying to abandon hope but rather to be realistic and pushing recovery is not realistic if it is not qualified.

The second problem was mentioned to me by my friend Kathy Mochnacki of Home on the Hill in Richmond Hill Ontario. She pointed out that if you claim that recovery is possible, then why continue doing research. People can recover so no need for it. Of course, scientists know better but they are dependent on funding from governments and other agencies.

So, let's all inject some scientific reality into a very troubling and serious disease.

Are Psychologists Over Educated Bartenders?

By Marvin Ross

A rather provocative title but that is the gist of a new book called *Psychology Gone Wrong: The Dark Side of Science and Therapy.* The book is written by Tomasz Witkowski and Maciej Zatonski, two Polish scientists who argue that psychotherapy is a business and a kind of prostitution rather than an effective evidence-based medical treatment.

Witkowski is a psychologist, science writer, and founder of the Polish Skeptics Club while Zatonski is a surgeon and researcher who debunks unscientific therapies and claims. Their book was reviewed by Dr Harriet Hall on the blog Science Based Medicine.

I'm pleased to hear them call psychotherapy a business as that is a criticism that I've lodged against psychology in a couple of my earlier Huffington Post Blogs. In one, I quoted an internal paper I came across from the Canadian Psychology Association. They were concerned that an emphasis by government on treating serious mental illnesses would mean an exclusion of mental and behavioural health which is their domain.

In my second, I suggested that there is a turf war between psychology and psychiatry with psychology trying to gain more clients. If we don't call psychiatric illnesses an illness but a mental health problem, then it becomes more appropriate for other professionals like psychologists to be the first line of assessment and treatment. Interestingly, psychologists are lobbying to prescribe medications and can do so in three US States. Likely, some of them seem to realize that their own theories may be deficient.

The authors point out that psychotherapy has been unsuccessful. Most of what psychologists do lacks proper evidence. Psychologists are still fixated on childhood trauma as the precursor to personality and as the cause of mental disorders. The only way to treat these mental disorders is with psychotherapy which depends on the reconstruction of childhood experiences. That is the concept underlying a great deal of their theories of problems like schizophrenia.

This concept, they argue, is dangerous and has led to the abuses of the recovered memory movement. In fact, the repressed memories are often the creation of the therapists themselves. Suggesting that schizophrenia is the result of childhood trauma and possible abuse serves no purpose other than to vilify the parents of offspring who are sick through no fault of anyone.

I made reference to bartenders earlier because the common perception that many have is of the wise and friendly bartender providing a sympathetic ear for the problems of his/her patrons and offering sympathy and support. The authors point out that conventional psychotherapy offers no additional benefits to that of a sympathetic friend. That is something we all need and those who are experiencing a serious illness need even more.

My own very special psychologist is Dr Bonnie Kaplan of the University of Calgary. For years, she has been pushing the use of vitamins for mental illness. She now begins her presentations with a warning to her audience with "Don't Google My Name" as she did twice in this presentation in Syracuse.

Part of the reason she wants no googling is that two of my colleagues and I have been very critical of her vitamin research over the years. She went so far as to file a formal complaint against physician Dr Terry Polevoy with his regulatory body for unprofessional conduct arguing that he had no right to criticize her research. It was thrown out.

And what purpose does telling people not to google them have? We all know that human nature will only result in the opposite happening. Seems that she fails to understand basic human psychology.

Harambe the Gorilla and Mental Illness

By Marvin Ross

Like many, I was saddened to see Harambe shot. Was he helping the toddler as the initial photo may have suggested or was the toddler in danger as the subsequent video suggested? I have no idea! But I am astounded that there are seven petitions out there for people to express their dismay. One petition is approaching 500,000 signatures as I write this while another is getting close to 200,000 signatures.

That's a lot of people who want justice for the gorilla.

Sadly, there is far less of an outcry when someone with untreated mental illness gets shot by the police. According to the Washington Post, a quarter of those shot by the police in the US were mentally ill. In Canada, according to a recent documentary on police shootings, 40% of those shot by the police are in a mental health crisis.

Here is one example of Toronto Police shooting a poor man in his hospital gown after he ran out of hospital https://www.youtube.com/watch?v=RbWUnzvAgb4

Shootings of those with untreated mental illness is only one small part of the injustices suffered by those who develop a mental illness in our society. In Canada, 38% of incoming prisoners suffer with a mental illness. Their offences often result from a lack of proper treatment. In Ontario, 40% of prisoners in solitary were locked away for 30 or more straight days. This is twice the limit permitted by the UN in its Nelson Mandela Rules. The main reason for the solitary was mental health or special needs.

Homelessness in Canada is accounted for by mental illness or addiction in between 23 and 67%.

In the US, a recent report found that there are 10 times the number of mentally ill in prison than in hospital. The consequences of not treatment, according to the Treatment Advocacy Center is homelessness, incarceration and violence.

And so few people care about any of this! Instead, we angst over one shot and killed gorilla.

To paraphrase Stalin one dead gorilla is a tragedy, a million maltreated and ignored mentally ill is a statistic.

Isn't it time we showed some compassion for the mentally ill and gave them appropriate treatment and support?

One Step Forward, Two Steps Back – Mental Illness Treatment Over the Past 150+ Years – Part I of IV

By Dr David Laing Dawson

In 1843 Dorothea Dix wrote: "I proceed, Gentlemen, briefly to call your attention to the present state of Insane Persons confined within this Commonwealth, in cages, stalls, pens! Chained, naked, beaten with rods, and lashed into obedience."

And so began the development of asylums for the mentally ill in North America, and the Moral Treatment era. Dorothea had learned from the Quakers in England, and some reforms taking place on the continent, and had brought those experiences and her prodigious outrage back to North America. We were ready for these ideas, as they arrived amidst a developing belief, a new conviction that the "state" should bear some responsibility for the care of those among us who cannot care for themselves.

This was truly a new idea, and one that was transforming the Hotel Dieu in France into the General Hospital, transferring responsibility for the indigent and insane from religious orders to the state.

We were also beginning to notice that not all the indigent, the incapable, the socially dependent among us were the same. Perhaps some were simply lazy, a few others without morals and scruples, but many were insane, others mentally handicapped, and some were incurable inebriates. The latter three categories did not deserve the neglect, the punishment, the harsh treatment that befell them when lumped with the former two categories.

(The first building on the grounds of what was to become, eventually, Hamilton Psychiatric Hospital, was an institution designated for incurable inebriates, a branch of the Toronto Asylum for the Insane).

For the most part, with a few setbacks here and there, the next 150 years after Dorothea's proclamation heralded incremental progress in the enlightened treatment of mental illness, mental handicap, and addictions. Science brought us more understanding of each form of mental illness and mental handicap, and, eventually, some medical treatments that are actually effective. In poor economic times and times of war (1914 – 1918, 1929 – 1939, 1939 – 1945) we neglected our growing, burgeoning institutions for the mentally ill and the mentally handicapped. Conditions deteriorated in each of these eras, and I'm sure some abuses occurred. The discharge rate was understandably very low during the 1930's. But for all their failings, these now enormous asylums, with their own kitchens, farms, food production and laundries, set in the rural surround of our cities in North America, at the end of train lines in England, and on the banks of rivers in Australia, provided three meals a day, a chapel to pray in, grounds to walk on, and a bed to sleep in. But during peaceful and better economic times we paid attention. Conditions were improved in the 1920's, reforms instituted within the knowledge and philosophies of the times: airing courts, more freedom, activities, visitation, better food, entertainment. And after the Second World War a new era began, one of hope, stability, idealism, and new convictions about rights and freedoms.

The first medications that actually helped depression, that controlled mania, were introduced in the 1950's; the first medications that actually worked with psychosis, with schizophrenia, were introduced in the 1960's. Rehabilitation, work programs, activities, music, exercise, social programs. Our academic institutions, medical schools, psychiatry departments, began to pay attention to these large asylums and their populations of seriously mentally ill, oddly neglected by academia the previous 50 years, save for field trips to demonstrate catatonia, mania, hebephrenia, and dozens of rare but severely disabling and disfiguring forms of congenital abnormality.

I stepped into one of these institutions in 1968 as a first year resident, along with three other young doctors and two associate professors of psychiatry. It was one of the acute admission wards serving Greater Vancouver, men and women, dormitory sleeping quarters, a brightly-lit day room, spacious grounds, forty patients, but just one component of a large mental hospital comprised of several enormous buildings, some from the Victorian era, this one built in 1931, originally for WWI veterans, all perched on a hillside overlooking Coquitlam and the county of Essondale. We unlocked the door; we instituted "community meetings" every morning, a quasi-democratic reform and a chance to air grievances. We prescribed the new drugs for mania, schizophrenia, and depression. But when someone was well enough to be discharged we had no community treatment programs and support programs to refer them to.

Clearly this was the next thing that needed to be developed.

One Step Forward, Two Steps Back – Mental Illness Treatment Over the Past 150+ Years – Part II

By Dr David Laing Dawson

In the spring of 1969 a new psychiatric facility was opened on the campus of the University of British Columbia, the first component of a full service teaching hospital. This clearly heralded the future of psychiatry and the treatment of the mentally ill, or so I thought: a large outpatient department, space for a day hospital, and small wards for inpatients, wards for only 20 patients each, wide corridors, accessible nursing station, private rooms for some, no more than two to a bedroom and bathroom, earth-coloured patterned carpeting, earth-toned walls, residential style beds, comfortable furniture, warm lighting, pleasant dining room, a sitting area with lounge chairs and fireplace, meeting rooms, no locks on the doors. Even sliding doors to small balconies for many rooms occupying the ground and second floor.

Perhaps there was not quite enough security to manage the most disturbed, potentially violent patients, but it is really a small percentage of the mentally ill who do not respond well to treatment offered in a non-threatening compassionate fashion within a very comfortable environment. The impulse to flee is actually reduced when the door is open. The impulse to say NO is reduced when the treatment is offered gently and patiently. The impulse to rant and break things is reduced when the lighting is soft, the chairs comfortable, the colours soothing, the sounds not echoing off concrete walls. The impulse to hit someone is greatly reduced when that someone is not threatening you.

We were experimenting with forms of something we then called "The Therapeutic Community", which really meant open meetings of staff and patients sitting in a big circle each morning, discussing everything from housekeeping issues to medications to ward rules and protocols, to the question of whether or not one patient should go off his medications or take more, and if another is ready for a weekend pass. It wasn't thought of as "the treatment" but rather as a humane and democratic context for treatment, and an environment that would bring out the best in people.

It is true we were reading Thomas Szasz, R. D. Laing, Jay Haley, Erving Goffman, Michel Foucault, Gregory Bateson and all the others postulating that the roots of madness could be found in distorted parenting or unbridled capitalism or imposed social conformity, but you really don't have to spend much time with someone in a manic state, a stuporous depression or an active schizophrenic psychosis before you know, as a colleague once succinctly put it, "It's a brain thing."

My next stop was England, to see first hand a large mental hospital that had eliminated locked doors altogether. Serving Cambridge and the surrounding shire it sat brooding on the fens just as you and Thomas Hardy would imagine, a large winged Victorian mansion with a few marginally more contemporary buildings around it. It was, by North American standards, poorly resourced, under-heated, and I was quickly appointed physician to six wards of forty patients each. But the doors were all unlocked; each ward had its daily community meeting, its occupational therapy programs, good nursing and medical care, grounds to walk on, work to do, social and entertainment programs. It was an asylum, a humane asylum, and proof of a sort that decent psychiatric care did not require modern buildings with state of the art security.

Still, it can be assumed, (and my personal survey supports this) that everybody, every patient, would prefer to live and be cared for in his own home rather than in any kind of institution.

It was 1971. We now had effective treatment for most psychiatric illnesses (not all but most). It was time to build an array of outpatient, community, and home treatment services that might gradually reduce reliance on mental hospitals.

One Step Forward, Two Steps Back – Mental Illness Treatment Over the Past 150+ Years – Part III of IV

By Dr David Laing Dawson

Part II ended with the phrase: "gradually reduce reliance on mental hospitals." "Gradually" is the operant word here, even though, as I recall, during the kinds of planning workshops, conferences, meetings we had in those days, at least during the "visioning" part of the exercise – the "vision thing" as George H. W. Bush once called it – some of us imagined a day when mental hospitals would no longer be necessary.

From 1971 until 1995 I worked in a variety of settings, sometimes as a participant, sometimes as a leader, developing comprehensive outpatient programs for serious mental illness – programs for schizophrenia, supported housing, programs for mood disorders, programs for early detection and comprehensive treatment, programs for brain injury, for crisis intervention, programs for isolated regions, programs for consultation to medical wards and family doctors. We revamped the mental hospital, transferring more and more funding to outpatient services, redefining "chronic ward" to rehabilitation program, reducing the use of restraints. We worked at connecting with school and social services, housing and job training.

Still, for some people, the mental hospital remained an asylum, the one place in the world where they were safe, could eat meals and sleep in a bed, could receive medical and nursing and dental care, could sit in the sun on a bench, have a shower, cadge money from the medical director for a coffee, and wander about in eccentric fashion making outrageous observations.

And someone mentally ill in the jail on minor charges might be transferred to the hospital without a great deal of fuss. Some fuss, but not a great deal. Police would apprehend someone creating a disturbance, observed to be mentally unbalanced in some way, and bring that person to the emergency department, to the emergency psychiatric team rather than the jail. They would have to sit around for a bit to await outcome, but they could usually count on the hospital keeping that person and they could get back on patrol.

Government policy shifted focus and money from the worried well to those suffering from severe and persistent mental illness.

Better treatments were being developed, more money spent on research; our country was not at war, the economy was growing, more people were being educated, the digital age arrived, information became readily available. This era of progress could only continue, one would think.

Of course the new drugs proved only marginally better than the original mood stabilizer, the original anti-depressant, and the original anti-psychotic. Talk therapies were being refined, codified, made more practical, but they too did not add much more than having an empathic, nonjudgmental, reasonably wise counselor in your corner. Yet the world was becoming a better place for the mentally ill and their families, at least my part of the world, and much of Europe, and parts of the United States. Surely this progress would continue and Dorothea Dix, Drs. Pinel, Kraeplin, Tuke, and Rush would be pleased.

During the latter part of those years, I attended a psychiatric conference in San Francisco. I was probably there to talk about comprehensive treatment for schizophrenia. But what I remember most clearly is the number of homeless and psychotic people living on the streets near the hotel and convention headquarters. An ironic tableau: a thousand psychiatrists within, a hundred mentally ill living on the streets outside, and a few people picketing with anti-psychiatry placards. Another psychiatrist from another state (I think it was Georgia) came to give a talk in Ontario during that period. He came with a warning. Do not let happen in Canada what was happening in his country. His hospital, the mental hospital in which he had worked, in which he had pursued all the same goals mentioned in that second paragraph of mine – it had been closed and transformed into a medium secure prison facility for the mentally ill and criminally insane.

One Step Forward, Two Steps Back – Mental Illness Treatment Over the Past 150+ Years – Part IV

By Dr David Laing Dawson

It is difficult, if not impossible, to fully understand the forces altering, changing, insidiously impacting our attitudes, laws, institutions, and behaviour in our own time. It takes distance and serious historians to dissect these things, and even then we are probably viewing them from a clouded contemporary prism. But something happened between 1990 and 2015 I would not have expected in 1970. Many of our mentally ill fellow citizens today are worse off than they would have been had they been born 50 years earlier. There are parts of the United States where one could make the case that they are worse off than they would have been had they been born in 1850. How could this have happened during a period of increasing knowledge, advanced medical tools, relative peace and prosperity?

This is one part of the puzzle:

The mental health laws were tightened, restricted during those years (1970 to 1990), and safeguards put in place, all toward the righteous goal of preventing anyone, ever, from being unnecessarily stripped of freedom and independence without "due process". On paper it looks fine. Now one could not be held for a psychiatric assessment unless he or she was judged to present an **imminent** threat of harm to self or others. Within 72 hours if a psychiatrist came to the same conclusion about imminent threat to self or others, that person could be kept for another two weeks. Further safeguards were put in place – appeal processes, Review Board Hearings, lawyers made available, patient advocates. The wording, the processes are all a little different in each North American jurisdiction, but with similar intent and outcome.

And then the act of treating was separated from the act of detaining. A second process is required for involuntary treatment: a determination of not being competent to consent to treatment, and then the treatment authority would be conferred on a nearest relative, or, failing that, a public official. And this determination could also be appealed, taken to a Review Board, and ultimately to court.

This distinction between the right to detain and the right to treat has led to some paradoxical situations in which everybody loses. A person can be deemed too imminently dangerous to self or others to set free, to be allowed to leave, yet competent to refuse treatment. The patient suffers physically, mentally, left in a state of psychosis for a long period of time; families watch this suffering; unhappy doctors and nurses watch someone deteriorate to a state of chronic psychosis, to a state of true madness and unpredictability not seen in our mental hospitals since the introduction of effective medication.

Apart from this paradox all the new rules sounded commendable, and guaranteed to reduce or eliminate type I errors. Type I errors being the unnecessary detention of someone eccentric, a nuisance, but not dangerous, and the forced treatment of someone who should (within our current view of individual rights) be allowed to decide for himself. They prevent the abuse of a Nurse Rached, or a Dr. Donald Cameron. And these new rules were informed, to some extent I am sure, by our increasing awareness of the use of Psychiatry in the Soviet Union to deal with people deemed to be enemies of the state.

We need strong safe guards in all our systems and institutions, for humans in positions of power are always capable of abusing or misusing that power, of convincing themselves on some philosophical basis or other, that they are doing the right thing.

But when we completely eradicate the possibility of type I errors we open the door for type II errors. In this case not detaining someone who, in hindsight, should have been detained, not protecting and treating people who need treatment and protection. The most dramatic form of Type II error brings about the headline that we have read with horror and disbelief about twice per year the past twenty years. A patient is released from hospital, gets on a Greyhound bus, and decapitates a fellow passenger. A young man stops taking his pills and butchers his mother; another shoots a journalist with a crossbow; yet another shoots an Arizona politician in the head.

But a less dramatic and more insidious type II error has been the increasing numbers of mentally ill (not deemed imminently dangerous to self or others) left to fend for themselves on the street, in shelters, and in jails and prisons. For a significant number of mentally ill people (and their families) we have, over the past 30 years, reversed the reforms provoked by Dorothea Dix in 1843.

One Step Forward, Two Steps Back – Mental Illness Treatment Over the Past 150+ Years – Part V of IV

By Dr David Laing Dawson

Since writing Part IV, I've read E. Fuller Torrey's *American Psychosis*. So there is my historian tracing the manner in which the personal struggles of politicians, the belief systems of leading professionals of the time, egos, idealism, personal tragedies, and, of course, power, politics, and money brought about the disastrous transformation and destruction of the mental illness treatment system from 1963 to present time in the US.

Canada is always a slightly more cautious, reticent, little brother too often lead astray by his risk taking, grandiose big brother. We are not as enamoured with the profit motive; we have evolved a somewhat different social contract; our minimum wages and safety nets are better; our Federal Government dare not (thanks in large part to Quebec) tamper with social and health programs long the responsibility of our provinces (or initiate something unilaterally that would undermine or destroy Provincial Programs). So we still have most of our mental hospitals, and they are mostly linked and associated with our community programs. Our psychiatric leaders and teachers remained a little more grounded in the observations of Dr. Kraeplin than the fanciful extrapolations of Drs. Freud and Laing. We realize, I hope, that privatizing our garbage collection (providing we retain sensible unions) might be both fiscally and socially responsible, but privatizing the care of the mentally ill is not.

Yet in our own slow and cautious way we are following the same path as the US. Completely discredited ideas about the causes, treatments, and "prevention" of serious mental illness, once promoted by the Psychoanalysists who designed the American Community

Mental Health Programs of 1960 and 1970 are finding their way into our commissions and planning groups. Our linguistic avoidance of 'illness' in favour of 'issues' and 'health' is just another form of denial of the knowledge that, unfortunately, God help us, no matter how well we conduct our lives, we (and our children) can still be stricken with serious diseases of the body and brain. And, our cherished belief in inclusiveness, our understandable distrust of authority, even of scientific authority, and our wishful thinking and politeness, often allow equal voice to the speakers of nonsense on our commissions and task forces.

Much of the care of the seriously mentally ill has shifted to psychiatry programs and inpatient units of our General Hospitals. These are not for-profit institutions, but neither are they asylums; short stays are the goal; turn-over is rapid, and the doors we unlocked in the 1970's are once again locked. (Security becomes paramount when the unit is situated on the fifth floor of a General Hospital next to the surgical suite and the Pediatric ward.) Overwrought privacy laws allow health personnel to avoid the onerous task of talking with families and other caregivers. Time consuming and difficult appeal processes facilitate psychiatrists prematurely discharging very ill people who are not, strictly speaking, imminently dangerous to self or others.

We too now have mentally ill homeless, and jails and prisons with burgeoning populations suffering from mental illness.

(I remember being mildly astonished, in perhaps 1990, to find that an Ontario Ministry of Health task force, seeking to determine the optimal number of psychiatric inpatient beds per 100,000 population, was using the State of Georgia as a benchmark. Not The Netherlands, Finland, Sweden, Denmark, but Georgia. It is sometimes difficult to resist American enthusiasm.)

We have had the opportunity of adopting some of the good and effective programs pioneered in the U.S. (the ACT programs) and avoiding some of their bad ideas; we are developing a number of programs to help the police (now often front-line mental health workers by default) in many jurisdictions; we have some means of mandating forced community treatment for those who remain at risk (though it is underutilized).

Still, our development of community programs to service the

seriously mentally ill has definitely not kept up with de-institutionalization. We seem to be, once again, inexorably following the misguided steps of our big brother to the south.

But, we have not destroyed our mental illness treatment system, merely hobbled it. So, in theory at least, as a country with a smaller population than California, we should be able to fix it.

Should We Bring Back Mental Asylums?

by Marvin Ross

Dr Dawson provided an excellent history of how much we have regressed in our treatment of those with mental illness in his five part series. Despite better (but not perfect) medications, and greater knowledge of the brain, we have, as he said, "For a significant number of mentally ill people (and their families) we have, over the past 30 years, reversed the reforms provoked by Dorothea Dix in 1843."

Certainly, the statistics for Canada, the US and the UK, bear this out. The Canadian Journal of Psychiatry pointed out that there was a rapid closure of beds in the 1970s and 1980s but that was offset by an increase in days of care in the psychiatric units of general hospitals. They called this transinstitutionalization. But, by the 1990s the overall days of inpatient care began to decrease. Between 1985 to 1999 there was a decline of 41.6% in average days of care per 1000 pop in psychiatric hospitals and a decline of 33.7% in psych units in general hospitals. Days in hospital declined but there were more frequent stays for patients – the revolving door.

In a document by the Public Health Agency of Canada called the Human Face of Mental Illness, it was stated that "This discontinuity and inadequacy of care after hospitalization is common among seniors who have lived with schizophrenia for most of their lives. After being transferred from psychiatric institutions they may find themselves in long- term care facilities that generally have limited availability of mental health professionals."

Meanwhile, there was a near-doubling in the total proportion of prison inmates in Canada with mental illnesses between 1997 and 2009. Prisoners often end up in segregation units and without adequate treatment because the prisons don't have the staff or resources to properly care for them.

In the US according to the Treatment Advocacy Center, in 1955 there were 340 public psychiatric beds available per 100,000 U.S.

citizens. By 2005, the number plummeted to a staggering 17 beds per 100,000 persons. And we know that the largest psychiatric facilities in the US are the jails in New York City, Chicago and LA.

The Guardian newspaper in the UK recently reported that more than 2,100 mental health beds have closed since April 2011, amounting to a 12% decline in the total number available. It also found that seven people had killed themselves since 2012 after being told there were no hospital beds for them.

On one occasion last year, there were no beds available for adults in England.

In 2011, Dr Peter Tyrer, a professor of community psychiatry at the Centre for Mental Health at Imperial College, London, wrote in the British Medical Journal that "I am now rueing the success of the community psychiatric movement in the UK, where the inane chant of "community good, hospital bad" has taken over every part of national policy. At some point in the steady reduction of psychiatric beds, from a maximum of 155 000 in 1954 to 27 000 in 2008 the downward slope has to level off or rise."

Meanwhile, earlier this year, three medical ethicists at the University of Pennsylvania, Dominic Sisti, Andrea Segal and Ezekiel Emanuel, argued for a return of the mental asylum in the Journal of the American Medical Association. They said that their use of the word *asylum* wasn't meant to be "intentionally provocative."

"We're hoping to reappropriate the term to get back to its original meaning, which is a place of safety, sanctuary, and healing, or at least dignified healing for people who are very sick."

The United States, they said, now has 14 public psychiatric beds per 100,000 people, the same as in 1850. On average, Sisti said, countries in the European Union have 50 beds per 100,000.

On a personal level, author Katherine Flannery Dering whose book Shot in the Head discusses how she and her 8 siblings cared for a brother with schizophrenia, described the impact of what she called The Great Emptying on one of the talks that she gave. As she says, the number of people needing hospitals did not shrink as much as hospitals did.

Asylums (or psychiatric hospitals) do not have to be evil places where patients are abused or ignored. There is no reason they cannot be caring compassionate places that give patients the necessary time to heal or to protect them from the outside world if that is what they need.

A Subjective Unscientific Analysis of Anti-Psychiatry Advocates

By Marvin Ross

Many of my Huffington Post Blogs attract some very nasty comments from the various anti-psychiatry adherents. The same applies to the blogs by my colleague Susan Inman and we get some on this blog. The Boston Globe award winning Spotlight Team featured in the film Spotlight, just did a series of articles on the sad state of mental health care in Massachusetts. Wanting to foster dialogue, they set up a Facebook Page for comments. And did they ever get comments!

I've been looking at more than my fair share of these comments over the years but decided to try to categorize them. So here goes.

1. I was badly treated, mistreated, misdiagnosed therefore all of psychiatry is evil. In some cases, this alleged mistreatment occurred over 50 years ago. I do believe that this happened in most cases and it should not have happened but it did. Personally, I've run into (or family members have) some very incompetent and inept treatment by doctors and/or hospitals. This has occurred in inpatient stays, visits to doctors or in emergency rooms. And some of these misadventures have been serious but I do not spend my time denouncing all hospitals, all doctors or all Emergency Rooms. What I have done is to complain to the appropriate authorities. And most of the time I'm successful.

As my English mom used to say, "don't throw the baby out with the bathwater"

2. The other very common cry is that I got help and recovered therefore everyone can recover and if they can't, it is because the docs are bad or are trying to keep people sick to make money and peddle drugs. I'm sure there is an error term in logic where you extrapolate your particular situation to everyone. That is what these critics are doing. It is like saying I survived prostate cancer which has a 5 year survival of 98.8% so that someone with pancreatic cancer can too. Pancreatic cancer only has a 4% 5 year survival rate. It is not the same nor is say mild anxiety comparable to treatment resistant schizophrenia. Stop mixing apples and oranges.

3. Involuntary treatment for those who are so sick that they pose a danger to themselves, others, or will deteriorate further without involuntary committal means that the state will lock up, drug and keep everyone indefinitely. None of these fears are true so learn what is entailed and get over it. And when I post a video or an article by someone like Erin Hawkes who went through about a dozen involuntary treatments till a pharmaceutical agent was found that removed her delusions, stop insulting her as some have done by calling her a victim and that she is suffering from Stockholm Syndrome.

How will you learn if you refuse to listen to other opinions?

What I suspect that these involuntary opponents do not understand is that people are not locked up without just cause or forever. There are safeguards in place to ensure regular reviews and appeals. In Ontario a few years ago, a group of so called psychiatric survivors challenged the constitutionality of community treatment orders and supplied the courts with affidavits from people who found them to be bad. This is what I wrote about that in the Huffington Post:

Justice Belobaba only had to look at the affidavit that the plaintiffs filed as part of their attack on CTOs to get an idea of how well they can work. Amy Ness had, prior to being put on a CTO, been involuntarily committed for showing violent behaviour in 2004. In 2007, while hospitalized, Ms. Ness kicked her mother in the back and hit her repeatedly. Then, in 2009, Ms. Ness grabbed a large kitchen knife and marched upstairs toward her mother after discovering a magazine about schizophrenia. In another incident, Ms. Ness kicked and punched the emergency department psychiatrist. By the time she was given a CTO in 2009, she had five hospitalizations.

Since then, while on a CTO, the judge pointed out, she takes her medication and sees her case worker on a regular basis. She has not been hospitalized, she maintains her housing and she works as a volunteer, has a job and takes courses. She does think, however, that the CTO is an attack on her personal dignity.

Herschel Hardin, a civil libertarian once wrote that:

"The opposition to involuntary committal and treatment betrays a profound misunderstanding of the principle of civil liberties. Medication can free victims from their illness – free them from the Bastille of their psychoses – and restore their dignity, their free will and the meaningful exercise of their liberties."

A psychiatrist I know who is a libertarian (someone who believes that people should be allowed to do and say what they want without any interference from the government) told me that when your brain is immersed in psychoses, you are not capable of doing or saying what you want. Therefore, he was fully supportive of involuntary treatment so that people could get to the position where they had the capacity to do what they want.

4. And then we come to what Dr Joe Schwarcz on his radio show, Dr Joe, calls scientific illiteracy. He used that in his July 10 interview with my colleague, Dr Terry Polevoy, in a discussion on EM Power + and the conviction of the Stephans for failing to provide the necessities of life for their child who died of bacterial meningitis. They refused all conventional medical care, gave him vitamins, herbal products and echinacea till the poor little toddler stopped breathing.

There was a case of scientific illiteracy in that the parents are totally opposed to vaccinations and work for a company that encourages people with mental illnesses to go off meds in favour of their proprietary vitamins. They had no idea why they were convicted, lashed out at the jury who convicted them and then, at their sentencing hearing, the wife shocked even her own lawyer when she told the court that the Crown had used a phony autopsy report as evidence.

Other examples are that anti-depressants cause violence and suicide. Violence possibly in those under 24 according to a large Swedish study but not in adults. However, the authors state that these findings need validation. There is no definitive proof of this and **no evidence of increased violence in adults.**

As for anti-depressants causing suicide, a warning that this might be a concern was posted on the labels. Doctors were advised to be cautious when prescribing these for depressed young people.Consequently, this resulted in an increase in suicide attempts.

"Evidence now shows that antidepressant prescription rates dropped precipitously beginning with the public health advisory in

March 2004, which preceded the black box warning in October 2004. Since the initial public health advisory, **antidepressant prescriptions for children and adolescents decreased, with a consequent increase (14%) in incidence of suicide in these populations."**

On my to-read list is *Ordinarily Well The Case for Antidepressants* by psychiatrist Peter D Kramer. Kramer is the author of *Listening to Prozac* and, in this new book, he continues with proof that antidepressants do work and are not simply placebos. Not only do they work, but they are life savers.

In the New York Times review by Scott Stossel, the reviewer points out that when Kramer first began visiting psychiatric wards in the 1970's, they were filled with people suffering what was then known as "end-state depression". These were depressed patients in what appeared to be psychotic catatonic states.

Patients like that have not been seen for decades which he attributes to the aggressive use of antidepressants.

And, lest we forget, there is also the common view that the chronicity of psychiatric disorders are caused by the drugs that doctors force on their patients. People love to quote the work of Martin Harrow in Chicago but I suspect that many have not actually read his studies. Some people, he found, did better after going off anti-psychotics over time than those who continued with their use but that is not surprising. It has always been known that some people improve while others have chronic problems and still others are not able to be helped with anything.

What they do not realize is that in Harrow's study, **79 per cent and 64 per cent of the patients were on medication** at 10- and 15-year follow ups. And that Harrow points out that not all schizophrenia patients are alike and that one treatment fits all is "not consonant with the current data or with clinical experience." His data suggests that there are unique differences in those who can go off medications compared to those who cannot. And he points out that **it is not possible to predict who may be able to go off medication and those who need the long term treatment.** Intensified research is needed.

So stop with the reference to Harrow that no one needs meds. And stop also with promoting Open Dialogue when, first, it has never been empirically validated and second, many of their patients are on medication.

5. Regrettably, many of these people lack any civility whatsoever. People are entitled to offer their comments but they should not do so anonymously. And they should show some respect for those who have different views. I'm told that some have been banned from the Spotlight Facebook page and I've just banned one anonymous person who posts here for his/her personal attacks. I mentioned above that Erin has been called a willing victim and one who suffers with the Stockholm syndrome for her video and her article. Refute the points she makes but leave the insults aside.

And, one post that I removed from the After Her Brain Broke page on Susan Inman in response to he video What Families Need From the Mental Health System claimed that Susan keeps her daughter locked up and ill and that she likely suffers from Munchausen by proxy.

Has Mad in America Changed its View of Medication for Schizophrenia?

By Marvin Ross

For those of you not familiar with Mad in America (MIA), it is a US organization begun by journalist Robert Whitaker. He is the author of books that are highly critical of modern psychiatry and its reliance on medication particularly for schizophrenia. As they say on their website they "investigate the problems and deficiencies with the current drug-based paradigm of care."

I happened to come across this announcement on their site: "In *World Psychiatry*, two Canadian psychiatrists argue that the body of scientific evidence about schizophrenia shows that it is not a progressive illness and therefore we should have much higher expectations of full recoveries than we do." I was intrigued because one of the authors of this study is Dr Robert Zipurski of McMaster University in Hamilton, Ontario.

Once before, MIA cited a study by him that used quotes selectively. They implied that Dr Zipurski provided proof of the evils of antipsychotic medication. Their website stated "decreases in brain tissue volumes are attributable to antipsychotic medication, substance abuse, and other secondary factors." But, a careful reading of that paper found that when people discontinue medication early, the relapse rate is up to 78 per cent compared to 0-12 per cent for those who remain on medication.

MIA did not provide its own interpretation of this current paper which Dr Zipurski wrote with Dr Ofer Agid of the Centre for Addiction and Mental Health in Toronto. The two authors continue from the previous paper mentioned above and point out that:

Relapse of psychotic symptoms following a remission from a first episode of schizophrenia is also observed to occur in over 80% of individuals when studied naturalistically. This is largely attributable to **discontinuation of antipsychotic medication** rather than to the effects of an unrelenting disease process. The risk of symptom recurrence in remitted first episode patients receiving maintenance antipsychotic treatment is estimated to be in the range 0-5% in the first year of follow-up, compared to 78% in the first year off medication and close to 100% after three years off medication.

The authors then go on to wonder why outcomes are so poor if people have the ability to remain in remission. The reasons, they say, are numerous including the lack of services for these people or that they refuse treatment. Then, of those who are treated, about 20-30% are treatment resistant to the available antipsychotic medications. Others are non compliant with medication and so have relapses and re-hospitalizations. For others, their concurrent problems with alcohol, drugs, and other mental illnesses mitigate against retained recovery.

They conclude that while "there is room for debate about how recovery should be defined, it should be clear that most individuals with schizophrenia have the potential to achieve a stable remission of symptoms and substantial levels of satisfaction and happiness."

That stability, they say, can be achieved with antipsychotic medication. Physicians/scientists/psychiatrists who observed that this dementia praecox or group of schizophrenias appeared to be a progressive disease were observing people with this illness pre 1960 before anti-psychotics were available – they were not wrong or overly pessimistic as there were no effective treatments at the time.

And it does take time for science to recognize that if someone begins antipsychotics at about age 19 and remains on them along with good medical care, that they can get to old age and remain stable or even improve.

It is encouraging to see MIA recognizing the importance of drug treatment by their promotion of this paper.

Mental Illness and the Political Spectrum

By Marvin Ross

I have always been on the left of the political spectrum – more so in my student days – but I still consider myself left and vote for progressive ideas and progressive candidates. Progressive, of course, is a value laden term but what has baffled me has been the lack of progressive ideas by the left on mental illness.

I've just done a Huffington Post piece attacking the establishment of a scholarship in anti-psychiatry at the Ontario Institute for Studies in Education (OISE) at the University of Toronto. After it was penned but before it was published, I was sent a link to an article in Rabble.ca written by the founder of that scholarship, Bonnie Burstow, extolling the supremacy of Toronto academia in anti-psychiatry "scholarship". She equates this anti attitude for the search for social justice and as diametrically opposed to Toronto's Centre for Addiction and Mental Health.

Aside from caring for patients, CAMH has a research budget of $38 million a year, is a World Health Organization Collaborating Centre and home to the only brain imaging centre in Canada devoted entirely to the study of mental illness. Among the supporters and activists of anti-psychiatry, Burstow cites David Reville and Cheri DiNovo. Reville was a politician in the disastrous NDP government in Ontario headed by Bob Rae (1990-1995). DiNovo is also an NDP member of the Ontario Legislature.

For non-Canadian readers, the NDP is the Canadian version of a Labour Party.

That disastrous government in Ontario brought in legislation to establish an Advocacy Commission to protect vulnerable people and to promote respect for their rights. That, of course, is laudable but the bill was so flawed and cumbersome that it was immediately repealed by the Conservative government that replaced them in power.

The Ontario Friends of Schizophrenics (now the Schizophrenia

Society of Ontario), told the committee that:

"Ontario Friends of Schizophrenics has had dialogue with officials because we have been persistent and because we have done our homework in making some solid proposals for improvements in the legislation. We have been unable to meet with a single minister of the three ministries concerned, despite repeated requests and despite the fact that people with schizophrenia are one of the largest groups in the vulnerable population that will be affected by these bills."

They then pointed out that the bill excluded families; that it gave more power to the commission to enter someone's home than the police have; that the test of capacity was ability to perform personal care rather than understanding; the low standard of capacity; no provisions for emergency treatment; and too much power to the Consent and Capacity Board.

The Alzheimer's Society of Metropolitan Toronto was equally critical arguing that the new act penalized the family. Their presenter told the committee that:

"I have serious concerns about the prevailing use of unknown professional advocates with sweeping powers, heavy demands on their time, unclear qualifications and little accountability."

In Ontario, the only improvement to the Mental Health Act was brought in by the extreme right wing at the time Conservative government under Mike Harris. They have not always been that extreme and the word Progressive precedes Conservative in the name of the party. That improvement to the Mental Health Act was Brian's Law which enabled those with serious mental illness to be hospitalized if they posed a danger (not imminent as previously) and to be discharged from hospital under a community treatment order. They could live in the community provided that they were treated.

Only 10 members voted against the bill, 6 of whom were members of the NDP. The Health Minister after this was passed was Tony Clement who showed his support for those afflicted with schizophrenia by attending the banquet at the Schizophrenia Society of Canada annual conference when it was held in Toronto. As mentioned above, the schizophrenia group complained that no elected official would meet with them to discuss the flawed bill they were implementing. I have always had respect for Tony while detesting his ultra right policies further honed in the Federal Harper government.

The one member of the legislature who has done the most, in my opinion, to improve services for the mentally ill and the disabled was Conservative Christine Elliott. It was her pressure that resulted in the Liberal Government establishing an all party select committee to look at possible reforms. Despite an excellent report agreed to by members of all three political parties, nothing has been done. Sadly, she left politics after not winning the party leadership but she is the first ever patient ombudsman in Ontario.

And this regressive attitude on mental illness by the left is not unique to Canada. My advocacy friend, DJ Jaffe of the Mental Illness Policy organization in New York often comments that even though he is a Democrat, the most progressive people advocating for improvements in the US are Republicans. He is referring to a bill by Republican Congressman, Dr Tim Murphy called the Helping Families in a Mental Health Crisis Act. I suggested that Canada could use help in mental illness reform from a Republican back in 2013. In 2014 I wrote about how little we could hope for reform in Ontario.

To demonstrate further the left attitude to mental illness, you just have to look at the critical comments that my most recent blog on the anti-psychiatry scholarship garnered. One woman who is doing her PhD in Disability Studies at OISE claimed that I could not criticize because I am a white male member of the bourgeoisie. My proletarian father who worked in a garment factory on piece work and was a member of the Amalgamated Clothing Workers, would cringe in his grave located in the Independent Friendly Workers' section of the cemetary.

That criticism goes on, quoting Barstow, that all that is needed to cure mental illness is that those with the illness know "we are cared for and that we are in control of our own lives." Another critic said people "get better because they get free from psychiatry, find peers, get in touch with their inner experience, connect with and rely on others." That same person also said "Psychiatry was invented by the privileged to dehumanise (sic) women, the neurodiverse, gay and lesbian and transgendered people, the poor, the Indigenous, and never-to-be-heard survivors of child abuse."

I wonder how the scientists in the Faculty of Medicine or at the Centre For Addiction and Mental Health with their budget of $38 million a year feel about being told they are oppressors?

I haven't heard such rhetoric since the days of Trotskyites on university campuses in the 1960's but would love to see these critics spend some time in a psychiatric hospital ward with unmedicated schizophrenics, those experiencing the mania of bipolar disorder, or in a severe depressed state. I'm sure they would find some way to rationalize why their attempts to free them from "dehumanizing" psychiatry did not work.

Suicide Prevention – Thoughts For Practitioners

By Dr David Laing Dawson

I have written a blog before about suicide prevention, about many of the things we do that don't really make a difference, and about where we could and should put our resources if we want to make a difference. But this is a blog about suicide prevention on the ground.

We can talk about suicide prevention in general terms but the one and only time a health care clinician can actually prevent a suicide is when an at-risk individual is sitting in front of him or her. Your patient, new or known to you, at your office, in your clinic, at the hospital.

Some emergency and rapid response services have mandatory checklists. Most clinicians are taught to always ask the question. Many family doctors are fond of using a self-test for depression with questions like "Do you think of suicide?" with check boxes ranging from "all the time" to "never." And many clinicians contract with patients – that is they extract a verbal agreement from their patients to not harm themselves, at least not before calling.

My suspicion is that these activities provide a false sense of security for the clinician and do not necessarily make any difference to the outcome.

- While asking and focusing on the checklist questions and filling in the boxes, and taking notes, a clinician may well miss what I will discuss later.
- The direct question about suicide intent and suicide ideation yields far more false-positives than useful and truthful answers, to say nothing of a few false negatives.
- How we answer those self-test questions depends more on how we want to present ourselves to the doctor than a realistic appraisal of mental state, especially when it comes to the question of frequency and future behavior.
- And contracting with patients poses two problems: one is that it does not work. The other is a logical fallacy: If the clinician truly

thinks that the **only** thing preventing his or her patient from killing himself is a private promise that he won't, a promise that he won't let the clinician down, then that patient should be in hospital. And clinicians who contract in this way should think hard about the boundaries, the limitations, the nature and impermanence of the professional therapeutic relationship.

But day to day, mental health clinicians are faced with the difficult decision to act or not, with the anxiety of predicting human behaviour, in this case with a lethal outcome if they get it wrong.

Let me share with you what both good and bad experiences have taught me:

Rule 1: **Be present when seeing a patient**, be there, in the room, focused and attentive.

This may require, in many situations, a clearing of the head before entering the room, making sure other loose ends have been taken care of and are not nagging you. It requires an ability to be present in that room no matter how slow, painful, distasteful, or even boring the encounter is, or how many distractions insinuate themselves . **And it requires you to stay away from your computer screen, not take notes, and be quiet.**

Rule 2: **Talk less**. Empathy, the ability to experience what the other is experiencing requires silent observation, watching the eyes and mouth, the movement and posture, listening to the tone, the cadence, the intensity, the timbre, the intention of the spoken word as much as the content.

Rule 3: Without directly asking, **listen** for the presence or absence of future references in your patient's words, something he or she plans for next week, next year, tomorrow.

Rule 4: And lastly, watch for, listen for, **let yourself experience**, the presence of two emotions, the congruence of these two emotions if they are present:

Despair/hopelessness plus dread/anxiety.

If both of these are present this patient is high risk for suicide. And to know these are both there, residing in your patient today, you have to be there yourself, attentive, present, open, receptive.

The Mentally Ill in Prison – A Reply to the Centre For Addiction and Mental Health

By Marvin Ross

The chief of forensic psychiatry at Toronto's Centre for Addiction and Mental Health (CAMH) , Dr Sandy Simpson, gave his explanation as to why so many people with mental illness are in the correctional system in a blog earlier in December. I learned of it because a number of people contacted me upset by what he had to say.

He gave three main reasons for this phenomenon which you can read for yourselves. His first reason is the one that people found the most upsetting as he claims that "broken families, poverty, substance abuse in the home, physical and emotional abuse experience" are "problems that increase the risk of suffering a serious mental illness. Therefore people with problems of criminal behaviour may well also have problems of mental illness, but the illness is not the cause of their criminality."

This sounded like family blaming to those who contacted me and it does. I asked him on Twitter if he was suggesting that mental illness is caused by bad families? And I added, "Your point 1. MI in jail because of lack of services and beds". His Twitter reply was "Agreed to last point esp in US. Family one of many relevant factors for crime generally Family problems often social context driven". I then asked if he thought that serious mental illnesses were caused by families and he replied "no" but he did not reply to my tweet that his blog could be taken the wrong way.

His suggestion that the lack of beds might be a problem but that it is worse in the US is an interesting comment. That may be the case but so what? Is our negligence mitigated because someone else might be even more negligent? Imagine an accused murderer saying to the judge, "but your honour, I only murdered one person. Joe Blow murdered three people".

Now Doc Simpson works at CAMH and CAMH is notorious in my mind for refusing a court order to treat a mentally ill patient. In fact, they won a legal battle that prevents judges from ordering mentally ill offenders to be taken to a hospital for treatment. In 2010, Toronto judge Mary Hogan, was faced with a schizophrenic defendant before her on a minor offence. She ordered CAMH to stabilize him as she knew that the standard policy was that these individuals were rerouted to jail rather than hospital.

CAMH left him in the hall because they had no beds and initiated legal proceedings to prevent such orders. They won. Can anyone imagine refusing treatment to someone injured in a traumatic car crash because the hospital is busy? It would not happen.

Lack of adequate mental health services and beds is the main reason that so many with mental illness are in jail. According to a thesis submitted in 2011 to the University of Manitoba by Richard Mahé, it has been known since the 1970's that the lack of community resources resulted in the criminal justice system replacing the psychiatric hospital. The Canadian Institute for Health Information reported that the shortage of psychiatric hospital beds is resulting in people being squeezed out of hospital too early.

This closing of beds was decried by the Schizophrenia Society of Canada. And the Public Health Agency of Canada pointed out that "the rise in the proportion of prison inmates with mental illness suggests that some have exchanged the psychiatric ward for the prison ward."

Howard Sapers, the investigator for Corrections Canada, told the Tyee that "We've seen a big increase in the number of men and women being sent to federal penitentiaries with a mental health issue and many of them end up with diagnosed mental illnesses such as schizophrenia." And, he added, it is difficult to even find qualified staff willing to work in the prison system.

In fact, a state of the art infirmary and 26 bed mental health unit in the Toronto South Detention Centre has never opened due to a staff shortage. Inmates are being held in solitary confinement instead. Andre Morin, Ontario's Ombudsman, has threatened to intervene if the situation is not rectified.

So, Dr Simpson, there is a lot to talk about on the subject of mentally ill in jail that is a lot more crucial than speculating on the adequacy of families. And we have a lot of work to do to rectify that sad reality.

Family Day, Serious Mental Illness and Murder

By Marvin Ross

I'm posting this on Family Day in Ontario. This is a new statutory holiday promised by former Premier Dalton McGuinty during the election campaign of 2007. It was, of course, part of his platform so that he could win re-election by giving people an extra day off between New Year and Easter and sold as an opportunity for people to celebrate family.

Unfortunately, families with serious mental illness in them lost out when the recommendations of an all party Select Committee on Mental Illness and Addictions Report of 2010 was largely ignored by that government. There is little for many of these families in Ontario to celebrate as you will see from my Huffinton Post blog that follows. It was published on February 9 and I will update it at the end.

Was Ontario Complicit in a Father's Murder?

Last Spring, I mentioned the problems that a Richmond Hill, Ontario family was having with acquiring adequate service for their son with schizophrenia in one of my Huffington Post blogs. That was one of the many blogs I write on the pathetic state of care that we have for the treatment of those with serious mental illness.

Sadly, the father in this case, Bob Veltheer, was murdered on Sunday evening February 7 and, the next day, his son Jacob was arrested. Bob and his wife talked to me before I wrote the blog wanting to reveal just how badly people with serious mental illness are treated by the health system but decided to remain silent other than what I reported then.

Before I outline what I know of the care their son received, I should mention that Bob was the founding member and president of Home on the Hill, an agency set up to try to get housing for the mentally ill when their families could no longer keep them at home. I had been invited to speak at their monthly meetings a few times as had my blogging partner in another blog we share, Dr David Laing Dawson.

Last year, Jacob, who suffers from schizophrenia, was found sitting on a bus at the end of the line in Newmarket, Ontario presumably having failed to get off when it passed through Richmond Hill. He was suicidal, so the police were called and he was taken to South Lake Hospital. After a week and still suicidal, according to the family, he was discharged against the wishes of his family and that is what I reported.

Upon discharge, he ran off, as do many people with schizophrenia, and the York Regional Police went looking for him. He was found after three days and returned home only to disappear again. This time, when he was found, he was admitted to MacKenzie Health in Richmond Hill. After a brief stay, he was discharged with a community treatment order to a residence. A community treatment order is a legally binding order that the individual must accept regular medical help and medication. If they fail to abide by this, they can be returned to hospital by police.

Jacob, it seems, was too sick for the residence to cope with (but not sick enough to be in hospital) and was evicted from the residence. What should the parents do but what all parents do and that was to take him home. Just recently, the team that supervised his orders (the South Lake Assertive Community Treatment team), wanted him discharged to the care of the family doctor. His mother had just made contact with a local Richmond Hill psychiatrist and was waiting to hear back to see whether that doctor would see him.

Friday night, Bob had a meeting with a member of Home on the Hill executive at his house and I was told that Jacob was so distraught that he was pacing about the house talking to himself (or his voices or demons) in a loud voice. That Sunday night, the police allege that Jacob murdered his father.

This horrific tragedy could probably have been prevented had Jacob been kept in hospital long enough to stabilize him properly and, if that was not possible, to give him a secure place where he could live. The number of psychiatric beds in Ontario has been declining considerably over the past few decades but the total extent is not available since statistics on that can't be found. And I've tried. The most recent Ontario report released in December of 2015 called Taking Stock found that access to services varies across the province and is inconsistent.

Late last year, the brand new psychiatric hospital in Hamilton closed a ward because of budgetary problems although that hospital has 6 vice presidents, 31 directors, a medical director earning $500K a year and a CEO making $750K a year. And, as I wrote a year ago, Ontario has had 17 reports on the sad state of mental health care between 1983 and 2011 but little has been done.

This is not the first preventable death, nor will it be the last unless we finally start to care. In my book on schizophrenia, I describe a case where a family in Mississauga, Ontario desperately tried to get help for their son. They could not and he ended up killing both his parents. I met the son a couple of years ago and found him to be a very pleasant and sane individual. But that was after years in a forensic psychiatric hospital where he has been getting treatment. Imagine if his family were able to get that when they first tried.

I am not Emil Zola nor was Bob Veltheer, but I accuse the complacency of the Ontario government for his death. Government bureaucrats have been informed repeatedly both verbally and in writing about the need for accountability, program evaluation, transparency regarding mis-spending, mis-use of privacy legislation and the historical resistance to partner and collaborate with families. The Central Local Health Integration Network where Bob resided, I'm told, had recently been notified about the profound need for hospital beds by Home on the Hill.

Home on the HIll has been attempting to meet with the new Health Minister, Jane Philpott, whose constituency is near Richmond Hill but have not heard back yet.

I would like to see either a Coroner's Inquest or a Royal Commission into the circumstances that led up to this horrific event. And I would like to see Ontario finally do something other than commission studies which they then ignore.

Update

This blog received a great deal of attention as it was distributed widely and to a number of politicians where the Veltheer family live. I attended the funeral on February 13 along with politicians from the all three levels of government. The local town councillor who is a supporter of the work of Home on the Hill plans to bring this to the attention of the Ontario Minister of Health as is the local representative in the Ontario legislature. The representative who sits in the Canadian House of Commons is planning to raise this event in the House of Commons and a meeting has been arranged with the Federal Minister of Health.

We all hope that Bob's death and the pain that his family is going through will result in some positive changes. Ontario which has direct responsibility for providing health care needs to get off its duff, stop generating reports which they ignore, and start providing the services that have been recommended so many times by so many reports.

The Federal government needs to take the money they are wasting on a Mental Health Commission that has no direct authority and does nothing but generate its own reports and put it to providing funding programs in the provinces. And just maybe, Prime Minister Justin Trudeau whose mother, Margaret suffers with bipolar disorder, will understand and do something.

Doing something would be a welcome change and would honour the memory of Bob and all the others who have been sacrificed by our lack of resources.

Conspiracy Theories, Big Pharma and Anti-psychiatry

By Marvin Ross

The world is full of conspiracy theories from President Obama was not born in the US and is a Muslim to vaccines cause autism, cancer could be cured but Big Pharma prevents the cure to make money and Big Pharma drugs people with mental illnesses to also make money.

The only truth in any of that is that Big Pharma's goal is to make money. And that goal to make money is why they exist as they are private for profit companies in our capitalist society. TV networks, publishers, banks, retail outlets are all designed to make money by providing something that people either want or need.

What's the big deal?

And if you are opposed to that concept, then join a political movement that advocates for socialism. However, bear in mind that only Big Pharmaceutical companies have the means and motive to invent, study, produce new and better treatments for our ailments. But they need to be monitored, regulated, and whatever research they sponsor that "proves" the safety and value of a new agent needs to be replicated by independent studies.

Profit companies provide a service or a product that is needed in order to make money for their shareholders or owners. In the case of Big Pharma, it is medications that will help to ameliorate illness – probably not cure but reduce symptoms. They are the ones who do this because governments either can't or won't. History has shown that their products have dramatically improved our lives, or at least the levels of health and wealth and comfort that many of us maintain.

The role of governments is to provide a regulatory framework to ensure that these capitalist outfits do not ignore ethics in their pursuit of profits. Restaurants need to abide by rules of cleanliness for example so that their customers do not get ill and there are government inspectors to ensure that. In order to drive a car, you need a license as proof that you are capable.

The banking system requires very stringent regulations to ensure they do not run amok which is what happened to cause the recession in 2008. Many of the banking controls in the US had been removed and we saw what happened. Canada, which has always had a very tightly regulated banking system, was only mildly impacted by the 2008 crash.

And so too Big Pharma. In the US, Teddy Roosevelt brought in legislation creating the FDA in 1906 to regulate food and drug purity. At that time, many medicinal elixers contained opium, heroin and cocaine so regulation was implemented to make these products safer. Today, the FDA regulates drug development via a very stringent process to ensure that when a drug is made available to the public, it has proven to be efficacious for its intended purpose with side effects that do not outweigh its benefits. Absolutely we should not trust them or the doctors who shill their products for big paychecks. But without them there would be no pharmaceutical progress.

In Canada, that role is carried out by Health Canada and in the European Union, it is the European Medicines Agency. Each agency must approve any drug sold in that jurisdiction so that Big Pharma must gain the approval of the FDA, Health Canada and the European Agency to sell their product in those jurisdictions.

And drug development is expensive. It is estimated that for every 5-10,000 agents that begin preclinical testing, only one ends up approved for dispensing. The cost of developing that one prescription item is about $500 million and takes 8-12 years. That is a lot of money and time to get to market. Now I'm not justifying the price of drugs but the company does have to get its money back and show a profit.

The resources required to accomplish all of this are far greater than governments can afford. For those who think that drugs are mostly poisonous and are foisted upon unwitting patients by evil people to make money, this is the process to ensure that the drugs are as safe as possible.

Promising therapeutic agents are identified based on the latest understanding of a particular disease. That agent is then tested in lab animals to determine safety before an application is made to the regulatory body for an investigational new drug license. At this point, the testing involves 3 phases of study. The first involves giving a small amount of the agent to a small group of healthy volunteers to see if there are any adverse effects.

In the second phase, a small group of subjects with that disease are studied to see how effective the agent is. The third phase, if they get that far, can last for years and involve thousands of patients in various locations to test for efficacy compared to a placebo or an already approved drug and side effect profile.

Only then, years later, is the drug submitted for approval to the regulatory agency who then have their own scientists evaluate all the data. A drug approved by one regulatory agency for a particular country as I said earlier will also have to be approved the same way by the regulatory agency in those other countries.

This is a very long and costly process to ensure that the drugs doctors use for their patients are effective and have a side effect profile that is not greater than the benefit they have. And everything has a side effect including something as seemingly benign as water

Of course, it isn't always possible to predict what will happen when patients begin taking medications in the real world and so regulatory agencies do have adverse event reporting systems in place to track and investigate these occurrences. In many cases, drugs are removed from the market for various reasons that became clear with widespread use over time. Wikipedia has a very long list of these agents, the countries where they were pulled and the reasons.

The system is not perfect but it works for the most part and people are able to have prescription products to help ameliorate their symptoms. To attack Big Pharma for developing these drugs and the doctors who prescribe them for their patients, is absurd. I am not defending Big Pharma or suggesting that they do not sometimes go to excess but simply describing what is and why.

Thoughts on Schizophrenia Awareness Day – The Courage of Those Who Suffer and Their Families

By Marvin Ross

Every year, the World Health Organization celebrates October 10 as World Mental Health Day to raise awareness and this year their theme is living with schizophrenia. I think we should all pause for a moment and consider just how hard it is for those with this terrible affliction to cope and to commend them for how many of them do cope.

Imagine being a teen just starting out in the world and learning how to cope when gradually you start to become withdrawn, you likely hear strange voices insulting you and telling you to do various things, your reality becomes altered and you're not sure who your friends are and you begin to misinterpret their intentions and the intentions of your own family.

One of the best depictions of what it is like to have these delusions was by Erin Hawkes who described them to a conference on psychosis at the University of British Columbia in Vancouver last year.

http://www.bcss.org/recordings-project/2013-clinical-neurosciences-recordings/erin-hawkes-die-girl-die-my-psychosis-and-its-treatment/

But if the symptoms are not bad enough, those who suffer have to contend with the lack of understanding that so many have of schizophrenia. It is not a moral failure. It is not the result of bad parenting. It is an illness like so many other illnesses and those who suffer deserve to be treated with the respect accorded anyone else who suffers.

And they deserve to get a quality of treatment that others who are ill receive and that includes hospital beds when they need them, proper medical care, psychiatric care, support services like counseling, housing and vocational help.

The bravery of those who cope is exemplified here https://www.youtube.com/watch?v=4loR-bAKbuQ

And, we cannot forget to mention the family. It is devastating to any parent to watch the potential that their teen posses shattered by a horrific brain disease and the lack of sympathy that they often receive from those around them. As Katherine Flannery Dering put it "My younger brother Paul was more than a 'schizophrenic'. He was a brother, a son, and above all, a person that my eight siblings and I loved."

So, the next time you see a disheveled street person mumbling away to no one, remember that they are someone's child and they are likely sick and in need of help.

A Psychiatrist Looks at Recovery And Finds it Wanting

By Dr David Laing Dawson

There is something to be said for challenging our attitudes and shaking up our systems every decade or so, trying to improve them. Improve them, review them, discuss them, reorganize them, improve them. Even if it is really only putting old wine in new bottles. The new bottles can create a buzz, some excitement, add some energy, or, to use one of those terrible management phrases, achieve "stakeholder buy-in."

But language is important, especially when we use unassailable words, feel good words to hide something quite different. The Pro-Life Movement. Who could object to that? Until you realize it is really an anti-choice movement, and that it ignores the reality of the suffering and deaths of millions of young women around the world.

And in all our systems, not least in Mental Health and Mental Illness treatment, we are fond of forming a myriad of committees and steering groups, planning groups, focus groups that create a language of their own, and formulate, vote on, and sanction such meaningless phrases as,

"Co-occurring issues and conditions are an expectation, not an exception.
The foundation of a recovery partnership is an empathic, hopeful, integrated, strength-based relationship.
All people with co-occurring conditions are not the same, we all have a responsibility to provide co-occurring capable services.
When co-occurring issues and conditions co-exist, each issue or condition is considered to be primary.
Recovery involves moving through stages of change and phases of recovery for each co-occurring condition.
Progress occurs through adequately supported, adequately rewarded

skill-based learning for each co-occurring condition or issue. ”

–and then, on paper, design the most cumbersome and impossible organizational structure to carry out this mission, this formulation.

I get tired just thinking about it.

Usually such organizations and arrangements are wasteful but benign and fall by the wayside in a few years. But a few can be both wasteful and destructive.

Now the “recovery movement”, or “recovery model.” Who could object to the word “recovery”?

Until you look closely at it’s origins and implications.

It comes from addiction services, their philosophies and jargon. An alcoholic who no longer drinks is “an alcoholic in recovery”, or a “recovered alcoholic.” Similarly an addict. It is a useful term used in that context, I think, for it implies quite reasonably that if the alcoholic no longer drinks he is recovered, but still vulnerable. His recovery may end if he takes glass to mouth. And it also implies, quite clearly, that reaching that point of recovery and maintaining that point of recovery is primarily his own responsibility, an acknowledgement that ultimately he, the alcoholic, has the power within his own hands (with a little help from his friends) to choose to be and stay “recovered”.

But the “Recovery Model” as it crept over to mental illness, carried with it an anti-medical tone, a clear implication that we doctors and nurses did **not** pursue a goal of recovery for our patients. We were in the business, it implied, of maintaining illness, and thus maintaining our positions of power and our paychecks. A trifle insulting to say the least.

I, and all the people in our professions I know, are delighted when one of our patients really succeeds. Drops back to visit after graduating from High School, or University. Comes in to show me her brand new baby girl. Comes in and says, “I’m doing fine doc, just need my prescription renewed.” Sends me a card from his travels in Europe.

Well, I can get over the insult and their pejorative use of the term “medical model”.

It is those other implications of “the recovery model” that can be quite damaging. It does carry an implication, as with alcoholism, that the mentally ill person, this person suffering from schizophrenia, has within his own hands, his will power, the way he conducts his life, the means to "recover." It implies that those who don't recover are simply not trying hard enough. It implies that if you have to take a lot of drugs to stay well you are not trying hard enough. And, it must, by it's own convictions, ignore, banish from view, those with very serious mental illness who can hope for some quiet, some peace, some contentment, some happiness, some dignity, a relationship, some activity that gives them a sense of value, but never full recovery.

We would all like our patients to recover, to become well, to be able to live full lives with minimal suffering. Fine. But the "Recovery Model" with its emphasis on hope and prayer and peer support and its mantra that everyone can "recover" (with hard work and a little help from his friends) provides a foundation of easy denial for our politicians, our civil service, and our managers.

Often, through history, one can find that the theories of the day, regarding the human condition, are really rationalizations, comforting explanations for the terrible realities of the day. The Recovery Movement is a theory, a formulation, a rationalization for this day. It allows us to believe all mentally ill could get well if they really wanted to, just as all alcoholics could stop drinking if they wanted to or had to (with a little help). It allows us to ignore the millions of mentally ill now living in our prisons and flop houses, on the street and under bridges.

Towards a More Honest Interpretation of Schizophrenia Recovery

By Marvin Ross

Listening to an interview that Katherine Flannery Dering did last week about her book *Shot in the Head A Sister's Memoir, A Brother's Struggle* reminded me about how our emphasis on "recovery" in schizophrenia can actually hurt its victims and their families. As she explained in her interview, Ms Dering's brother, Paul, was one of the many for whom recovery was and is a dream. Perhaps it is time that we applied some reality to schizophrenia outcomes before we wave the recovery flag for everyone. By not doing so, we make those with a horrible disease and their families suffer even more.

The professional version of the Merck Manual which is a highly respected medical source for all illnesses states that "Overall, one third of patients achieve significant and lasting improvement; one third improve somewhat but have intermittent relapses and residual disability; and one third are severely and permanently incapacitated. Only about 15% of all patients fully return to their pre-illness level of functioning."

These outcomes have not really changed much over the years although, as a UK source states, "Early intervention and more effective treatment mean that the outlook is not as bleak as it once was." Still, why do we act as if everyone is going to get completely better?

The term recovery does tend to imply that the person is cured. Recovery in schizophrenia is defined by the Scottish Recovery Network as "being able to live a meaningful and satisfying life, **as defined by each person,** in the presence or absence of symptoms".

The goal **for each person** should be tempered by the reality of their situation. For someone like Ms. Dering's brother, over time, they realized that the best the family could hope for was stability and compliance with the rules of his group home. Yet too many in the mental health community tend to set up "recovery" meaning "completely better" as a universally achievable goal. And then when the majority do not, and cannot achieve that goal, they and/or their doctors are deemed to be deficient.

There was and probably still is a concept for breast cancer that suggested that group therapy helped women with breast cancer to cope and live longer. This concept became quite popular with the 1990 publication of a book called *Love Medicine and Miracles* by Dr Bernie Siegel. Those concepts were subjected to considerable scientific study and I had the privilege to interview a group of women with stage 4 metastatic breast cancer who had offered to be in a clinical trial to test this. It was the most difficult interview I've ever done.

The women all knew they were going to die soon and all of them said how much they hated Dr Seigel. They said that they knew they were dying and that no amount of group therapy, imagining that their cancer cells were being destroyed by their thoughts, relaxation exercises or meditation was going to change that. And, while they did not want to die, they felt that theories like those of Siegel suggested that if they did not get better it was because they did not work hard enough at the exercises.

Not only did they have terminal cancer but they were made to feel that not getting better was their fault.

The American Cancer Society states "the available scientific evidence does not support the idea that support groups or other forms of mental health therapy can by themselves help people with cancer live longer." It is cruel to suggest otherwise.

Similarly, when we hold up as achievable what 15 or 20% of those diagnosed with schizophrenia can attain as a goal for everyone, we do a disservice. Our goal for recovery should be for each person to be able to get the full range of treatment available so that they can achieve as much as they themselves are able to achieve.

On ECT, Jack Nicholson and One Flew Over the Cuckoo's Nest

By Dr David Laing Dawson

In my addendum to Marvin's blog last week I referenced Jack Nicholson in *One Flew Over the Cuckoo's Nest.* I'm sure everybody got the reference. Some of those scenes are burned into the collective imagination. And I was a fan of both Ken Kesey's novel and the movie. I say 'was', because as great as Nicholson's performance, as great as Milos Forman's direction, and Louise Fletcher's acting, the movie may have played a minor role in the demise of the Mental Illness treatment system of North America and a return to incarceration in jails and prisons for thousands of the mentally ill, to say nothing of an unwarranted negative public reaction to ECT. At least unwarranted since it has become more selectively and carefully used to treat only patients with severe illness not responding to medication.

The novel rose out of Mr. Kesey's part time work as an attendant on the night shift of a Veteran's Hospital, while taking part in a CIA sponsored experiment with psychedelic, hallucinogenic drugs, in the late 1950's.

Movies are magic, and they play fast and loose with the truth. In the sound and fury of them, in our vicarious pleasure of escaping our bonds, seeking revenge, getting back the man or woman of our dreams, and saving the world, we often miss a few nuances and incongruities.

Randle McMurphy does embody the free rebellious rule-breaking individual confronting oppressive institutional authority as personified by Nurse Rached. And the movie makes us root for him and hate Nurse Rached. Her ultimate weapons being ECT and Lobotomy.

Now there certainly is some truth to those big overcrowded wards of large mental hospitals being run by nurses whose prime directive was to keep everything peaceful, under control, with a modicum of care and nurturing on the side. And the doctor often was, as described by sociologists, the absent father whose power could be invoked by the nurses, as in "You just wait until your father gets home."

But here are some of the nuances in that film that slip by us: All but a couple of the patients on that ward are voluntary and could leave any time they wanted. And McMurphy, well, he is a charming psychopath, and he has faked insanity so he could be transferred to that hospital from a prison. His most recent conviction is for statutory rape with his defense being, "She came on to me." That would imply that McMurphy had sex with a 13 or 14 year-old child at the time the book was written.

Our attitudes have shifted a little since that film was made. Today McMurphy might be charged with "sexual assault" "rape of a minor" "sexual molestation of a minor". He would be placed on a sexual offense registry, and the public and our courts would show him little sympathy. And, I suspect, that if I were asked to provide a psychiatric evaluation of McMurphy, I would be telling the court that he is high risk to re-offend.

On the other hand, if any actor could make us root for a pedophile it would be Jack Nicholson in his prime.

Privacy Laws Should Not Exclude Families

By Dr David Laing Dawson

"Frustration over mental health disclosure doesn't trump privacy protection: experts" (CBC News, Halifax)

This story makes specific reference to a 21 year old who committed suicide after 3 trips to the University Health Services, only one of which her mother knew about.

Years ago, as a young psychiatrist with but one and then two very young children of my own, I am sure I "respected" the privacy of many of the teens I saw and treated. Usually our clinic staff saw them alone, and then invited the parent(s) in, and didn't disclose anything the teen adamantly refused to share. I can't remember the official age of consent at the time, but some years later it became 12. I remember this because a social agency asked me to see a 12 year old caught stealing. I said I would like to see his mother with him. They said, "We will have to ask his permission." My mouth fell open. "What? You need to get permission from a 12 year old before you talk with his parents? That is nuts."

Before that moment my thinking had evolved. Not least because I realized how outraged I would be if a doctor, counselor, psychiatrist did not tell me about important, serious things my daughter might disclose to her.

Working in a clinic that saw many teens, and consulting to local High Schools, I decided I could treat an 18 year old as an adult, and a 14 year old as a child. The child would always be seen with his or her parents. In between 14 and 18 the child had to prove he or she was "adult", in order to be seen alone. And by adult I mean have at least a rudimentary sense of personal responsibility, at least a rudimentary sense of the consequences of certain behaviors, at least a rudimentary sense of not being the center of the universe, at least a lessening of that knee jerk oppositional response to parents and any other authority, and at least a small decay in that adolescent sense of omnipotence.

Of course, within the first half hour of any interview most teens demonstrate that they are not adult in the above sense and then I would say, "I will have to talk with your parents."

They never fought me very hard on that because, really, they need and want their parents to know about their troubles. They want their parents to parent them. And that includes setting boundaries (protecting them) as well as loving and supporting them.

There was a time when I would ask a teenager something privately, working on the assumption that a.) In the presence of his parents he would not reveal the truth, and b.) His parents may not be ready to hear the answer. Sexual activity and orientation for example.

But my thinking evolved again. I concluded that, instead, a.) There is nothing I as counselor, physician, psychiatrist should know about a teen that his or her parents should not know and b.) Most family secrets are known or suspected by other family members already, and c.) If the parents have a bad, primitive, nasty reaction to the news, it would be better to have it in my presence.

So now I always see a child or teenager with his or her parent(s) and I ask whatever questions I need to ask. And I watch and I listen.

Occasionally I am talked into seeing a teen alone by a parent who insists I do so, and occasionally because the parent did not show up. It is always a futile exercise. It is not far off the metaphor of the blind man describing an elephant. There is one exception to this of course. Once in a while we run into a teenager who is more mature than either of her parents. In social work jargon, this is the 'parentified' teenager looking after the welfare and feelings of her parent(s).

I am talking about teenagers here, but it is not age that defines them. It is social, psychological, financial, emotional dependence on others. Their welfare depends on others.

But none of us is an island. Our health, our mental health, our welfare depends on others. So my policy of seeing teens with parent(s) has expanded to anyone who is financially, emotionally dependent on another. That includes college students, young "adults".

I am seeing them because they are in trouble. If the trouble has to do with drugs, alcohol, relationships, money, failing – parents are in a better position to help than I am, or, at least, their support is necessary.

If the young person suffers from a mental illness, then I may be able to treat that illness with or without the parents, but I want them informed and helping and supporting.

Health professionals put themselves in a bind when they see a young troubled person alone and he or she specifically says, "I don't want my parents to know."

To prevent that bind, privacy trumping parental concern and good care, we need merely see them together. The patient and his or her family. Together. In the same room at the same time.

So include them right from the beginning. Even bad parents, those who do all the wrong things (well-intentioned or not) should be included. For the child spends far more time with, is more dependent on, is more influenced by or reacting to, his parents than myself. Include them. Teach them if you can. Even if the teen objects before entering the interview room, persist, because he will change his mind very quickly once he understands he will be heard as well.

Don't give up on parents, family, until you see with your own eyes that they are hopeless, unhelpful, or destructive. When that is the case, unfortunately, we must counsel, treat, care for, look after someone who is not yet an adult as if he or she is a responsible, self-sufficient adult.

Suicide Prevention: In The Real World

By Dr David Laing Dawson

Marvin and I have written blogs about the failure of current and proposed "suicide prevention programs", the crisis line, the gatekeeper programs, the public awareness programs. He points out these programs make us feel like we are doing something, at least, but are a waste of money.

I would go further. I think they actually increase the number of people who use "suicide threats" as negotiating tools, and then through the intervention of family, counselors, and teachers find themselves in the Emergency Department of Hospitals being assessed by nurses, emergency doctors, social workers, and often the psychiatrist-on-call over a three hour to three-day period. This uses up our resources and poses the risk of inuring these front-line professionals to true suicide risk.

The number of people who actually kill themselves each year is remarkably stable. We know it goes down in wartime, increases in peacetime, and poor economic times. We know the demographics of suicide. We know the high-risk groups.

We know that a few of these suicides constitute rational, understandable, reasonable, sane and logical decisions to end one's suffering in the face of incurable disease and disability. Hence the current move toward allowing some physician assisted suicides.

We also know that the suicide of someone in other circumstances (temporary distress, intoxication, treatable illness) can be devastating to family and friends. It may in fact be an event from which a sibling, a parent, a child never fully recovers.

We know that many social factors put people at higher risk:

- inadequate housing,
- inadequate support systems,
- social isolation,
- bereavement,

- joblessness,
- addictions.

These factors have no simple solutions but can be gradually improved through well-funded social programs, retraining programs, affordable housing.

We also know that many suicides occur in the population suffering from severe mental illness especially when:

1. Discharged from hospital prematurely,
2. Unable to be hospitalized in a timely fashion,
3. Drop out of treatment or go off medication,
4. Their illnesses are not identified nor adequately treated.

We also know a particularly tragic circumstance is the suicide of a teenager, often responding on impulse to something they see as catastrophic, life impairing, hopeless, even while we adults know the situation is transient and will get better.

So what should we do if we want to spend our money on programs that will ultimately make a difference to that completed suicide statistic?

I don't think I can answer my own question in a blog, but I can start a grounded discussion.

1. Easy access to family friendly mental health resources including hospital beds.
2. Hospitals return to somewhat longer hospitalizations with discharge waiting until true stabilization and a good discharge plan. Stop the fast turnover and length of stay pressure.
3. Better comprehensive outpatient programs for the seriously mentally ill (including PTSD), ensuring the best possible treatment and compliance with that treatment.
4. Training, organization of services, physical environments that allow optimal detection and response to depression, anxiety and psychosis by family physicians and emergency doctors.
5. Continue improving our alcohol and addiction programs.
6. If there are to be government sponsored public education programs they need to counter the very loud voices denying the existence of mental illness, and denigrating medical treatment. They need to focus on parents monitoring their adolescents' online activity.

They need to focus on parents ensuring their adolescent does not have access to lethal weapons and substances.

As for the horribly high rate of suicides on our reserves and among our first nation peoples: I do not think they suffer from a higher rate of actual mental illness than the rest of our country. But all those social factors that increase risk are ubiquitous on many reserves:

- Alcohol and drug abuse
- Poor housing
- Poverty
- Severe unemployment and underemployment
- Poor rate of attendance and completion of school.
- Easy access to lethal weapons and lethal drugs.
- Social disintegration and corruption.
- The hopelessness and anger fueled by dependency.

We should study the reserves that are successful, and then work with the leadership of the first nations people to recreate these factors within less successful reserves. Throwing money at the problem does not help. Sending in more "mental health professionals" does not help. Responding to political whims and self-serving demands does not help. We need to help the leadership of these reserves find clear-eyed solutions or improvements to each of the social problems listed above.

The Word 'Issue' Has Become an Issue.

By Dr David Laing Dawson

There it was again. The local paper reporting on homelessness, reporting on the results of a survey of over 400 homeless people in our city. All very nicely written and laid out. The number of homeless people who have been the victims of violence; the number who struggle with addictions. And the over 80% who suffer from "mental health issues."

Dictionary definitions of the word 'issue' include:

"An important topic or problem for debate or discussion" – the operative portion of that definition being "for debate or discussion."

Now I understand that how we describe or name something may shift and change over time, often for good reason, often not. We no longer use the word 'retarded' to describe someone who has less than average intellectual capacity. It is a word that accrued a lot of baggage through the years, and became a schoolyard epithet, implying, at least in the vernacular of teenagers, something like "willful stupidity", or "in bad taste."

But euphemisms often creep into our vocabulary to hide the truth, or to reduce the sting of truth. Sometimes the euphemisms are simply more polite ('disability' may become 'special needs'); sometimes they are obfuscations with only a limited reference to the original activity, problem, or thing ('illness' becomes 'issue'), and sometimes they are softer vague words chosen to hide the reality of the action or intention of our governments, bureaucrats, and military, and sometimes they are even, a la George Orwell, antonyms of the word that would actually reveal the truth.

I don't know how the word 'issue' became the mot du jour, sometimes even added as a totally unnecessary noun. As in 'he has addiction issues' instead of 'he is addicted'. I suspect it is related to the actual meaning of 'issue', (a topic open to debate), and by calling mental illness an issue we are placating the deniers of mental illness and we are reducing it to an abstraction, a topic for discussion and debate, rather than a reality in our midst, and often the actual cause of homelessness.

Even if, reasonably, we want to reserve the words 'disease, illness, and disorder' for only severe forms of this reality, this plight, we still have other words to chose from that do not imply a debatable abstract: 'problem, difficulty, trouble, worry'. We might even say "mental health concerns, including mental illness".

But let's stop with the "issue" when we are naming or describing a painful reality.

Reforming Mental Illness Services is not Rocket Science

By Marvin Ross

Last week's blog in Mind You by Dr Dawson on rationally planning services made me realize that creating and implementing services for mental illness is not rocket science. Part of my realization arose from two psychiatric emergencies that my own family had to deal with in the past year. Both had fast and positive outcomes unlike so many others. The reasons, I think, are quite simple.

Starting at the front line of service for serious mental illnesses are the police. Every community needs (as my own community has) a police/psychiatric professional team to respond to emergencies. The city of Hamilton has a Crisis and Outreach Support Team called COAST. Their phone line is 24/7 but they also have a mobile team, consisting of a mental health worker, and a police officer, and will respond to crisis calls between the hours of 8 a.m. and 1 a.m. daily.

To supplement that, a properly trained police force sensitive to the reality of serious mental illness and with compassion is required. Yes there are exceptions that receive a lot of publicity but from what I've seen personally and from what people tell me, we mostly have that now. I am continually amazed at the extent that many ordinary patrol officers go, to help in these situations.

What many communities lack is an emergency department reserved for psychiatric patients and staffed by specialists which Hamilton does have. Of course, it has to be well integrated with the regular ER with considerable consultation so that people are not wrongly pigeonholed. As so many of you can testify to, the standard reception in ER is to isolate the psychiatric patient and keep them waiting. Then, they are more often than not discharged over the wishes of their family. If they are admitted, it is only for a brief period of time and they are not allowed to properly stabilize. There are never enough beds in most communities.

Recently, a young suicidal girl in Ottawa spent eight nights in the ER and was discharged because their were no beds. In Guelph, Ontario, the emergency room was brought to a standstill recently because there were so many psychiatric patients there waiting for the too few beds available for them. One mother in Vancouver told me how her son with schizophrenia was "tossed out of" an ER in Toronto as the nurse told the mother via long distance that all he needed was a sandwich.

And that is the other crucial piece – hospital beds. I'm fortunate to live in a community with one of the few stand alone psychiatric hospitals left in Ontario. There are beds and while there may be shortages, people usually get to stay if they need to in order to become stabilized. While not every community can have its own psychiatric hospital, they should have sufficient beds in other hospitals reserved for people with psychiatric problems.

Sadly, they don't and because of that people often get discharged long before they should as the pressure for more emergency beds increases. Thus, what we get are very sick people hospitalized long enough to take the edge off the worst of their symptoms and then tossed out so more emergencies can be handled. It is the revolving door that we have now. The Vancouver mother I cited above also told me that:

Ten years ago, again in Toronto, my son was turfed out of hospital (St. Mikes) after a couple of weeks, at night, into freezing February winter, with no money, no friends or relatives at hand ... nothing. It was a terrifying scramble for us, 3,000 miles away, to try to get him into a hotel so he wouldn't freeze to death on the streets. Looks like nothing has changed.

What is important for those who do have the fortune to stay long enough to be stabilized is to have a caring competent staff who treat them **and their families**. Hiding behind fake privacy to exclude families from treatment and discharge decisions saves no one other than incompetents who fear oversight. Finally, the last piece is proper discharge planning. No one should be discharged without a place to stay, follow up with an outpatient clinic or community medical staff, and sufficient supports to help them maintain their improvement.

When governments don't want to do something but want to give the appearance of doing something, they set up a task force or committee to investigate and bring back a report. It looks good to some but does nothing and that is what so many jurisdictions do. Maybe it is because I live in Ontario but this province is the master when it comes to this. Between 1983 and 2011, there have been 16 reports done by the Ontario government on reforming mental health care and few changes. I haven't bothered to add in all that has gone on since then but it would add to the numbers.

The solution is easy but getting there is not. We will only get there when we continue to press the politicians and drag them into doing what any civilized community should do and that is to properly care for those who are ill. And by that, I mean all the ill.

On Adolescent Suicide

By Dr David Laing Dawson

Adolescent suicide is a tragic event. It can have a devastating and life long impact on others: parents, siblings, teachers, relatives, counselors, friends.

Five Woodstock, Ontario teens have taken their own lives since January this year. A very high number for a small community.

If this were a cluster of deaths from respiratory causes we would surely investigate with a team comprised of a respirologist, an epidemiologist, and the public health officer.

Thus our first step here should logically be an investigation by an epidemiologist, a psychiatrist, and the public health department. Let us first see if these deaths are a result of undetected, untreated mental illness, if the teens know one another in real life or through social media, if they are all browsing the same toxic websites, or if each has been the target of bullying or something worse, or a combination of these. Let us try to understand before rushing into awareness programs, school assemblies, more crisis lines.

There are several good reasons to not rush to "talking about it" as the answer. These are teenagers, not adults. We know from anti-smoking programs, when we gathered our high school students into the auditorium to talk to them about the horrors of smoking and showed them videos of cancer-ridden lungs and COPD sufferers gasping for breath, the number of teens taking illicit puffs at the local smoking pit increased. **Increased. Not decreased, increased.**

We are also living with the paradox of contemporary times when kids are inundated with suicide awareness programs, when every school counselor and nurse asks every troubled kid the question, when each community has an advertised crisis line, when the question "do you ever think of harming yourself?" is asked on countless questionnaires and surveys, when our teens are communicating with each other around the clock, when information on any and every subject is as available as the nearest smartphone, and when we are in the midst of public discourse about assisted suicide. It is in these times, not in the 50's, 60's, or 70's (when the word suicide would only be said in the same whisper as syphilis), that clusters of teens are committing suicide.

Or so it seems.

But what I am trying to say is that we should investigate these phenomena before we rush to "solutions", especially with teenagers. They are not adults. They often do things just because they have recently learned those things are possible to do. They are often **more** intrigued when adults bend over backwards to warn them of danger.

The adolescent brain has lost some of the intuitive avoidance and fear of the child's brain. It is developing some reasoning and analytic processes to replace these. But it does not have the breadth and depth of experience of the adult brain, nor the ability to consider the distant future and the effect on others. The adolescent brain tends to live entirely within its present context.

"Would you swim with sharks?" When a child is asked this question he or she will answer with an emphatic NO. An adult will also offer a very quick negative, though with some adults and a few adolescents the questioner may need to add that 'sharks' is meant in a literal sense. But the teenager. Ah, the teenager. He or she asked that same question will ponder it. You can see and sometimes hear the analytic reasoning kicking in: "Well, humans are not the sharks' natural prey, so....and though I am not a good swimmer....and depending on..."

So far, with teens, my own informal survey has resulted in answers of "yes or maybe or I'd consider it" 100 percent of the time.

I am not saying we should downplay suicide and it's tragic consequences. I am saying that we should treat an increase, a cluster of suicides like any other serious outbreak of illness. We should study it without pre-judging. And when teens are involved we should take into account their contrary minds.

The Woodstock cluster may be a problem of inadequate resources; there may be a contagion factor at work; there may be a local stigma about seeking help; there may be some cyber bullying occurring; the means to kill oneself may be too readily available; there may be untreated mental illness involved; they may all have been fans of the same toxic Web site; they may know one another, or not; they may be using or misusing the same drugs; they may be all attending the same counselor; or this cluster might be simply a statistical anomaly...

We should help family and friends cope with these tragedies, but we should investigate before we plan a preventive intervention.

The Course of a Psychotic Illness – In Response to Psychiatry and the Business of Madness

By David Laing Dawson MD

In the late 1960's and early 70's when a young man or woman in a psychotic state was brought to the hospital by family, by ambulance, by friends or police, we would admit him and keep him safe. He would have a physical examination, some blood tests, and be fed, if he was willing to eat. If she was delusional, hallucinating, talking in an incomprehensible manner, we would optimistically hope that the cause of this was the ingestion of illegal substances, perhaps LSD, Mescaline, mushrooms. We would wait a few days before concluding otherwise. In fact, we sometimes waited one or two weeks, even three weeks, before concluding that this was a psychotic illness **not** induced by drugs. Drug induced psychosis actually clears quickly; it doesn't take weeks, but we might indulge in wishful thinking along with the boy or girl's family.

The history, the symptoms, the family history might clearly point to one of the psychotic illnesses studied and delineated over the previous hundred years (schizophrenia or manic-depressive illness), or not clearly one or the other, perhaps both. Nonetheless we now had effective treatment, drugs that actually work. These would be prescribed. And over the next few weeks to perhaps 8 weeks, our young man or young woman almost always got substantially better. The few that did not progress that quickly had been quietly ill for years before the admission. Average length of stay in the hospital grew shorter and shorter, at that time somewhere between 20 and 60 days.

But the other bit of folk wisdom with the backing of experience was that it usually took at least three admissions to hospital before such a patient achieved long-term stability. And this happened for four main reasons: we prematurely stopped the medication, severe side effects forced us to stop the medication, the patient stopped taking his medication, or the patient, stable within a quiet, supportive environment, entered a new, complex, chaotic and demanding environment that provoked relapse (a relationship, university, a job, travel, even a poorly considered therapeutic program.)

And throughout this process, the family, the patient, and the caregivers all struggled to find a way of understanding, talking about the illness, and finding a balance between cold truth and hope.

It often took three or four admissions before the patient and his family could come to terms with having a mental illness that required medication for a long time. This was not aided by our own optimism, our hope that a six or twelve month course of these very new medications would be sufficient to keep psychosis at bay for years to come.

What actually happened, inevitably, after stopping the medication, was a three or four or even six month period of wellness sans drugs, giving unfortunate support to the conviction of not needing them, followed by relapse of illness, of psychosis.

So these admissions and recoveries and relapses and re-admissions often spanned 5 to 10 years before stabilization was achieved. And, for those who eventually stayed on their medications, another 5 to 10 years of recovering the lost skills, the lost time, of learning what to avoid, of finding a way to live a full life with a chronic illness. Not least of those adaptations is finding a way of thinking about, accepting, as part of one's past and present, several periods of psychosis, of misreading the world, of damaging relationships and sense of self, of being delusional.

I have been living in and around the same city now for 45 years. And from that period in the 1970's I have known a few people who gradually made complete recoveries while consistently taking their medication, adjusted over time. And while they have recovered and lead full lives they know they are vulnerable; they know what to avoid; they know they must stick to some routines. I know others who take their medication and have achieved stability if by no means full recovery. And I know of others who have not, who have never been willing to take this medication over a long period of time. Some have died. A few others I see around town occasionally, one in a torn raincoat, walking down the center of the street gesticulating madly and talking to the clouds, another, a woman, standing outside a variety store haranguing exiting customers about incomprehensible injustices, and another plodding along the sidewalk, his head bent in unusual fashion, talking to himself.

But never, in those 45 years, have I seen someone who suffered from this kind of severe psychotic illness, recover fully without consistently taking his or her medication. You'd think by now, if it were possible, I would have seen it.

The Psychiatric Interview and the Biology of Mental Illness

By David Laing Dawson MD

I am tired of the mind/body argument, the dichotomy. I am tired of hearing about "new" models, theories, and psychotherapy processes, new gimmicks. I am as tired of the overreaching DSM IV and V as I am of mental illness denial.

Here is what a psychiatrist actually does, or at least what I do:

I read whatever information is given to me about the patient I am about to see. From this I am already formulating some lines of inquiry, some hypotheses to be considered. The one certainty at this moment is that I am seeing these people because they have a problem and they want help.

As my patient or family enters I am watching them, how they interact, how they sit, walk, speak, what their eyes are telling me. I say or do something to break the ice, from the weather to the news to the book the eleven year-old is clutching or the new Blackberry his mother is putting back in her purse, or the pink Samsung the teenager is holding as if it were a lifeline to planet Earth.

And then I ask questions and listen and watch. The questions are not random but neither are they detached from the reality in the room. Some are derived from science and experience, some from high and low culture; some are designed to ease my patient's or family's journey to full disclosure of the whole story. And right from the beginning and throughout this process I am asking myself if I should be thinking of this, this problem unfolding, as an illness, an illness derived from its biological origins, or as a psychological reaction to something, as a parenting or family problem, even sometimes as a broader social problem, a misfit of school and child, as a serious harbinger of a life long deficit, or merely a developmental stage, a passing thing, and even if it might really be no problem at all, just a bump in the messiness of life. And always, how much is this present realty, this "talking to a psychiatrist", impacting the story I am hearing?

Sometimes I know the answer to these questions by the end of the appointment. Sometimes I know that I will not know the full answer for a month or a year or two. Sometimes I fear I will never know.

But, far more importantly, I am also asking myself these questions: Is someone suffering? How badly is he or she suffering? Do I (we) have the means to alleviate this suffering? And my choice of the means to alleviate this suffering will depend on the patient and her family's feelings, thoughts, convictions as much as my own interpretations and conclusions. And of course, that prime directive, "Do no harm."

But, if you have sat on a mattress beside a young man in a full-blown schizophrenic psychosis, or paced the corridors with a manic librarian, or sat for any length of time with a woman in a state of agitated depression, or debilitating obsessions, you will know that a.) There is a lot of suffering here, and b.) These are brain things, biological illnesses.

It is not an uncomplicated matter. The modern concept of disease has only been with us a hundred and fifty years or so. And this very concept, this idea of disease, could well be the reason you are alive reading this now, and did not die from diphtheria, pertussis, polio, perhaps cancer – or be more crippled than you are with arthritis. It is also the concept that has allowed us to successfully treat severe depression, mania, psychosis.

I am sure some of my colleagues over-use the illness/disease concept when trying to understand a perplexing behaviour. And some I know under-utilize it. I'm sure I get it wrong sometimes. And many non-physician mental health workers simply apply the feel-good concept of the month, or bypass any attempt to understand the problem, it's roots and pathways, and focus instead on strengths and goals and those things that we all know contribute to a healthier life.

Fair enough. But instead of arguing about concepts of illness/disease/mind/brain/body, we should focus on relief of suffering, and helping someone return to a level of functioning he or she desires, and we should use all the tools in our tool box to accomplish this, providing we have evidence they actually work.

On the Efficacy of Suicide Prevention

By Dr David Laing Dawson

In the past decade, make that two decades, we have witnessed a plethora of mission statements, lectures, programs, public health campaigns, TV ads, crisis services, anonymous telephone answering services, crisis lines, websites, information initiatives, task forces, white papers, all aimed at suicide, reducing the suicide rate in our communities, preventing suicide.

Yet the rate of suicides in Canada, completed suicides, **remains statistically unchanged**.

All of the above activities make us feel we are doing something about the problem. We are trying. But that is all they do.

The problem with a public campaign to prevent suicides is that it is akin to a public campaign to prevent heart failure. Both are end stages of other processes, but in the case of heart failure we know enough to target smoking, cardiovascular disease, obesity, hypertension, diabetes, rather than "heart failure". We do not say, "Call this number if your heart is failing."

We know the demographics of completed suicide. We know the risk factors. We know the specific and usually treatable illnesses that all too frequently lead to suicide. So if we truly want to reduce the actual numbers of people who kill themselves (not threats, small overdoses, passing considerations), then we need to stop wasting resources on "suicide prevention programs" and put them into the detection and treatment of those specific conditions so often responsible for suicide:

- Some suicides are bona fide existential decisions, a choice to end one's life of suffering: terminal illness, intractable pain, total incapacity.
- Some suicides are the result of chronic complex social factors: unemployment, divorce, poverty, loss, alcoholism, addictions, isolation, and chronic illness. We can chip away at these factors with better support and rehabilitation services, improved minimum wage,

retraining – but there is nothing we can do quickly and easily.

- Some youth suicides are the result of impulsivity, intoxication, and an available instrument of death. Impulsivity comes with youth. Parents can keep an eye on intoxication. But we can make sure no instruments of death are available. Guns. Pills. Cars. Get rid of the gun(s) in the house. Lock up the serious drugs. Driving the family car is a privilege, not a right.
- Some teen suicides today are the result of public shaming, bullying. Watch for this. Chaperone the parties. Monitor Facebook, Snapchat. No cell phones or internet in the child's bedroom. It bears repeating: NO cell phones or internet in the child's bedroom.
- And then we have the specific mental illnesses that all too frequently, especially when undetected or under-treated, lead to suicide. These are Depression, Schizophrenia, Bipolar Disease, Severe Anxiety, PTSD, and OCD. And if we really want to make a dent in that suicide statistic then our programs, our money, our resources, should be directed to detection, comprehensive treatment, and monitoring of these illnesses.

Laying Bare the Sacrifices, Pain, and Even Joy of Caring for a Mentally Ill Relative

By Marvin Ross

Surveys of and anecdotes by caregivers tell of the extreme lengths that we all go to in order to ensure that our family members with serious mental illnesses are safe, cared for and are able to enjoy as good a quality of life as they possibly can. But *Shatterdays Bipolar Lives* by Frank and Melanie Shanty is the only book that I've ever found that lays bare the sacrifice that families endure beginning from the onset of the illness to, in this case, a premature death.

Susan Caltrider first became ill at age 14 and was diagnosed with schizophrenia and spent lengthy periods of time in various institutions. By 1976, doctors suspected that she had been incorrectly diagnosed, changed the diagnosis to bipolar type I with psychotic symptoms and started her on lithium which had just recently become available.

Susan's mother then spent the rest of her life caring for and overseeing her daughter's care and progress through numerous hospitalizations, encounters with the police and ensuring that she attained whatever benefits she was entitled to from the state. None of this was easy for her with four other children, a husband, a rocky marriage and a career. One aunt is quoted in the book saying that "when you have a special-needs child, they become your life". Melanie added that "without a doubt, this statement accurately describes my mother's relationship with Susan".

When Susan's mother passed away from cancer in 1998, Melanie, a year younger than Susan, took over her care. Melanie had promised her mother that she would assume the responsibility that her mother had shouldered since the early 1970s. "At that moment, I didn't realize the weight of that promise or the emotional toll it would eventually take on me".

Susan's social worker of many years is quoted saying that "Melanie's love for her sister was the game-changer. If you took Melanie out of the equation, Susan would have ended up on the street, a victim of violence or confined for a large part of her life. Melanie enabled Susan to have a life...."

That commitment to her sister came at a price that all caregivers of adults with serious mental illnesses can relate to.

"Although I felt a responsibility to Susan, she was a burden. The painful truth is that with the passage of time, I became resentful. I often wondered if I would be able to maintain my commitment to her. Although I had empathy for my sister, I found it harder to juggle career, family and serve as Susan's care provider. I was physically exhausted and emotionally drained"

"Counseling enriched my life beyond what I could have accomplished on my own. I am not who I was twenty years ago. But success wasn't easy. Frequent bouts of anxiety, anger and depression kept me in therapy during the thirteen years I was Susan's primary caregiver."

I won't go into the crises and challenges that occurred regularly as you can learn about those by reading the book but Susan did fare reasonably well and was married to a man with schizophrenia for many years until he passed away. Sadly,Susan's life ended too early in 2011 as the result of a fire in her apartment building.

In Melanie's ending words, Susan's "story resonates with 'ordinary people' caught in the throes of mental illness and provides a beacon of hope for caregivers. Susan's life was a testament to the power of love and commitment".

One aspect of the book that struck me was the care that Susan received from the medical system beginning in the 1970s and on. When needed, she was admitted to hospitals or care facilities and her stays were lengthy by today's standards. But then, towards the end of her life, Melanie took her to Johns Hopkins ER in a highly agitated manic state. Hopkins had access to her charts but all the doctor was concerned about was if she was going to harm herself or others. When Susan said no to both, she was not admitted and sent on her way.

Melanie commented that the doctor ignored her obviously elevated mood and “now believed that the mental-health barometer had changed from treatment to to crisis management – crisis defined as the desire to harm yourself or others”. She is right and it is now worse. Many families can attest to the difficulty of getting their obviously ill relative admitted and, if they do, the stay is not long enough to properly stabilize the person.

Because Melanie had her own business, she was able to employ Susan part-time for a period. Susan had previously worked for her mother two days a week and enjoyed that. The job with Melanie provided social interaction and the psychological benefit of feeling productive. Sadly, this is not something that most people with serious mental illnesses can acquire. Many are capable of part time work but there are very few opportunities. Instead, they sit around all day smoking and drinking coffee which does nothing to help improve their mental state.

Shatterdays Bipolar Lives by Dr Frank Shanty and Melanie Shanty is available at Amazon and other book sellers in print and e-book versions. I highly recommend it particularly as a book you can give relatives to help them understand your ill family member and how your life is impacted trying to help them.

What if Mental Health Awareness Was Successful – Chaos?

By Marvin Ross

Mental health awareness week/month/whatever is designed, in part, to reduce the stigma towards what is called mental health issues and problems – a politically correct phrase. One commenter on my last post that was skeptical of mental health awareness pointed out that stigma prevents people from seeking treatment. "If more individuals with mental differences (a politically correct phrase if ever I've heard one) seek help, they will be less likely to commit crimes, or end up homeless."

Let's say that's true. All those people who were afraid of stigma actually began to seek help. Where would they find it?

They won't because It is not there!

As I pointed out in my blog on Mental Health Awareness, the Mood Disorder Society of Canada found that 91% of people who were seeking help in Canada wanted to have greater access to professionals. Over one third had to wait for over a year to get a diagnosis.

This past winter, a 17 year old girl was discharged from an Ottawa hospital still suicidal after spending 8 nights in the emergency room waiting for a psychiatric bed. That same month, the emergency room in the Ontario city of Guelph was at a standstill because they had a psychiatric bed shortage. There were over 10 people in a psychiatric crisis with no beds for them. In Vancouver, a man is discharged from hospital early and given a bus ticket. Within an hour, he jumps off a bridge.

Inuk artist, Beatrice Deer has recently complained that "it was difficult to get therapy, because there weren't any therapists," as she pleads for a state of emergency to deal with suicides

In the US, the Substance Abuse and Mental Health Administration reported that only 35% of the reasons given for failing to seek help was because of what we could call stigma – negative opinions from others was at 10.6% and negative impact on jobs was 9.5%. The absolute biggest reason was that they simply could not afford to get help at 45.4%. A little over a quarter thought they could deal with the problem on there own.

What if the US had universal health care like other industrialized countries and cost was not an issue? From everything that I've read, they do not have sufficient resources. The Treatment Advocacy Center has begun a national campaign to lobby for more psychiatric resources in that country.

In Canada, we do have universal health care. Psychiatric services and hospital stays are free. The problem is that we do not fund psychiatric care to the same extent as we do other illnesses. In my last blog, I cited this from the Centre for Addiction and Mental Health in Toronto:

While mental illness accounts for about 10% of the burden of disease in Ontario, it receives just 7 per cent of health care dollars. Relative to this burden, mental health care in Ontario is underfunded by about $1.5 billion.

The provincial auditor in British Columbia has just released a report pointing out that mentally ill people in that province need more services than they are getting now.

So, let's forget about stigma and focus on getting proper funding for those who suffer from mental illness. A mental illness is no less worthy than cancer, heart disease or any other illness.

It's time for parity.

Mental Illness Literacy

By Marvin Ross

In a recent Huffington Post blog, Susan Inman (After Her Brain Broke: Helping My Daughter Recover Her Sanity), wrote about the need for greater literacy about mental illness. And, like me, Susan often gets inundated with comments from opponents. One was from John Read, a psychologist at the University of Melbourne.

Susan was arguing that we need greater understanding of the biological causes of serious mental illness and I agree. Read, however, commented that:

"The evidence is over 50 studies all showing that biological beliefs increase fear and stigma. I'm afraid you are swallowing drug company propaganda, there is no evidence that these drugs prevent violence."

When challenged to provide sources, he countered with:

"If anyone is interested in what the reserch (sic) says on this issue……

READ, J. (2007). Why promulgating biological ideology increases prejudice against people labeled 'schizophrenic'. Australian Psychologist, 42, 118-128.

READ, J., HASLAM, N., SAYCE, L., DAVIES, E. (2006).Prejudice and schizophrenia: A review of the 'Mental illness is an Illness like any other' approach. Acta Psychiatrica Scandinavica,114, 303-318."

In an article that I wrote for the World Fellowship for Schizophrenia and Allied Disorders in 2010, I mentioned the Read approach. Basically that approach states that we should ignore the illness in favour of viewing mental health problems as part of our shared humanity. One of the research papers by Read that I commented on was a 2002 paper which compared the biological explanation of mental illness to a psychosocial explanation. And while Read points out that the psychosocial explanation helped reduce stigma more that the biological, he admits there was no statistical difference between the two.

This is the link to his first article that he cited in his comments to Ms Inman. You can decide but note the lack of objectivity in his title.

Biological explanations are cited as **ideology** that are promulgated and **schizophrenia is in quotes**. The second paper he cited deals mostly with surveys asking people what they considered to be the causes of mental illness. Many of them believed that the causes were psychosocial which just proves that Susan Inman is correct in wanting to see greater literacy.

But again, to prove his point, he says that a study that showed a video of a person describing their psychotic experiences increased perceptions of dangerousness and unpredictability in viewers. However, a video explaining the same experiences in terms of adverse life events, led to a slight but non significant improvement in attitudes by those who viewed it.

Again with the non significance. It means there was no difference between the two. The responses were the exact same! Someone who acts scary and displays very abnormal and aberrant behaviour is going to be shunned regardless of the explanation for that behaviour. He does cite a number of papers but they date from 1955 to the latest in 2005.

In my 2010 article, I quoted Dr Heather Stuart, an expert in stigma at Queens University in Kingston, Ontario who said that there have only been six controlled studies of stigma. One of them by Patrick Corrigan found that education did lead to improved attitudes. I could not find a reference to that paper in the one by Read.

As an example, those with advanced symptoms of Hansen's Disease looked very frightening and were isolated from society. The Leper Colonies existed because no one understood the disease and were afraid they might get it too. But then, modern medicine came along, discovered Leprosy was caused by a bacteria, learned to treat it early and we no longer have people disfigured when treated early. We might still cringe at the thought of leprosy but likely no one has ever seen an advanced case.

In a similar vein, the solution for schizophrenia stigma is not to pretend it isn't what it is but to provide treatment. As Queen's University psychiatrist Julio Arboleda-Flores said in his 2003 editorial in the Canadian Journal of Psychiatry, "the best approach is to limit the possibilities for people to become violent via proper and timely treatment and management of their symptoms and preventing social situations that might lead to contextual violence;" he writes that "this could be the single most important way to combat stigma."

And one way to ensure that is to have greater mental illness literacy as Susan suggested.

Now I also have to comment on a post to Susan's blog by someone who is continually criticizing both Susan and I for our writing on the medical model for schizophrenia. Suzanne Beachy did post a number of comments which you can see for yourself but my favourite is her announcement that another critic of the medical model, Rossa Forbes, has just announced that her son is cured of his schizophrenia.

It seems that his cure was delayed by their being "sidetracked by institutional psychiatry perpetrating the false belief that there was something gone horribly wrong with his brain and only they knew the magic formula to set things right again." If you go to Ms Forbes blog, you will see her extolling how well her son now is which is wonderful. In fact, she says, he is so well that he has reduced his Abilify to half its dose and is planning to go completely off slowly over time. Abilify, of course, is an anti-psychotic used to treat schizophrenia and is prescribed by psychiatrists.

I am dumbstruck as I am with all the critics of modern science.

Exploring Delusions

By Dr David Laing Dawson

Well, let's talk about delusions. The word, as a verb, is used in common parlance as "You're deluded." or "He is deluded." referring to a mistaken belief, often one that will soon be proved wrong.

Much time is spent in undergraduate psychology, philosophy and medicine discussing, arguing about the concept. Could one man's delusion be another man's truth?

One could probably find more evidence to support the notion that the earth was populated by visiting spacemen a million years ago than the notion God created everything in seven days 4,000 years ago.

I suspect one would be hard pressed to find any man or woman out of our seven billion who does not hold to at least one irrational belief. Ghosts, lunar influences, karma, fortune tellers, telepathy, vengeful Gods, and ..... this list could go on and on.

So when is an irrational belief a delusion? More importantly, when does this phenomenon indicate illness, mental or neurological? When is it a symptom of illness?

And how does one decide this?

I suspect that the anti-psychiatry movement is partially fuelled by this fear. The fear that this group of professionals, working within a medical model, goes about arbitrarily deciding what belief is delusional and what belief is not. And each psychiatrist, being a member of one culture or another, will hold some irrational beliefs of his or her own, acceptable in that culture.

Karl Jaspers, psychiatrist and philosopher, defined delusions in 1903 as beliefs that fulfill these three criteria:

- certainty (held with absolute conviction)
- incorrigibility (not changeable by compelling counterargument or proof to the contrary)
- impossibility or falsity of content (implausible, bizarre or patently untrue)

All well and good until we come to the third criteria. Who decides, and upon what basis, the belief is implausible, bizarre, or patently untrue?

On the other hand, it is a very rare event for a psychiatrist to find out later that what he diagnosed delusional was actually true. And the reason for this is that Jaspers has ignored one other criteria for a belief to be considered part of an illness, an aberration of the mind/brain. And that is the manner the delusional conviction overrides all social realities and drives behaviour to destructive and self-destructive pathways and actions.

When talking with a psychiatrist a sane person, whether patient, friend or colleague, might preface a conviction with, "You will probably think I'm crazy but...". Whatever the belief (astrology, karma, ghosts), this person is aware, at the same time, of the present social reality, the possible or probable response of the other. He or she is sane.

But there is no preface for the delusional person. He or she will launch right into the conviction, either oblivious to the current social reality or unable to read it, or (delusionally) convinced that this idea he or she has will over ride, or somehow dominate this other reality.

Hence the young man, with both parents in the room with me, announces that he is "the illegitimate son of Adolf Hitler". (I wondered at the time why this delusion included the unnecessary word, 'illegitimate', but as with most delusions, the phrase, the words, often carry more reality than the inferred physical reality. Which is why, I think, that I have often over the years, been able to admit such a patient to hospital voluntarily. As long as I don't challenge the assertion with countering words, he will come with me to the ward and stay awhile.)

It is one thing to harbour a belief that perhaps you could survive on oxygen, water and the word of God alone, without food, but not mention this to your family doctor, your dietician, or test out this theory. It is quite another to wander into the woods, or travel to Alaska, to put this theory into practice.

It is one thing to harbour a pet belief that you are a descendent of royalty, while shopping, working and playing Canasta with your friends. It is quite another to introduce yourself as Queen Victoria.

So a delusion as a symptom of illness is all that Karl Jaspers described, but it is also a conviction that over rides current social reality, that obsessively dominates all thought and interactions, and puts self and others at risk.

Psychiatry, Eugenics and Mad In America Scare Tactics – Part I

By Marvin Ross

Much of what I read on the Robert Whitaker website, Mad in America, stretches logic but this newest blog has to be one of the biggest stretches I've seen. Dr Robert Berezin, a US psychiatrist, warns that psychiatry is moving closer and closer to eugenics.

As defined by dictionary.com *"eugenics* is a word that made everyone at the event uncomfortable. ... The very subject evokes dark visions of forced sterilization and the *eugenics* horrors of the early 20th century. ... The study of hereditary improvement of the human race by controlled selective breeding."

The most famous proponent of eugenics was Adolph Hitler who wanted a pure Aryan race but the subject has been advocated by many in recent history in an attempt to eradicate debilitating diseases. In fact, one could say that the reason for amniocentesis is to do just that. Sampling of the amniotic fluid of pregnant women can predict such things as Down's Syndrome. And some parents will opt for abortion if Down's is found but many do not.

Amniocentesis can also predict such genetic conditions as Tay Sachs Disease where the infant usually only lasts to about age 4. But, nowhere in the article by Dr Berezin does he actually show that modern psychiatry is planning to eliminate anyone who suffers from schizophrenia or any other psychiatric disorder.

What he talks about is the fact that genetics is being employed to try to understand these conditions better. He states that:

The accepted (and dangerous) belief is that psychiatry deals with brain diseases – inherited brain diseases. We are back to absolute genetic determinism. Today's extremely bad science is employed to validate not only the idea that schizophrenia and manic-depression are genetic brain diseases, but that depression, anxiety, phobias, psychopathy, and alcoholism are caused by bad genes

I have no idea why he considers the genetic research to be bad science other than he does not agree with it. So what if he doesn't. He does state that "The temperamental digestion of trauma into our personalities is the source of psychiatric conditions." But, as Dr David Laing Dawson has written on this blog:

Childhood deprivation and childhood trauma, severe and real trauma, can lead to a lifetime of struggle, failure, depression, dysthymia, emotional pain, addictions, alcoholism, fear, emotional dysregulation, failed relationships, an increase in suicide risk, and sometimes a purpose, a mission in life to help others. But not a persistent psychotic illness. On the other hand teenagers developing schizophrenia apart from a protective family are vulnerable, vulnerable to predators and bullies. So we often find a small association between schizophrenia and trauma, but not a causative relationship.

Dr Berezin's concern does not come from anything that anyone has said about aborting fetuses that genetic testing proves will be born with schizophrenia or bipolar disorder or any serious psychiatric condition. And the reason for that is that genetics and the understanding of the causes of these diseases is nowhere near a point that this can be demonstrated with 100% accuracy. Science is a long way from getting to that point if it ever is able to.

Suggesting that these research avenues will lead to abortion, eugenics or something similar is absurd and nothing but scare tactics perpetrated by someone who does not agree with the causation theories being investigated. If these avenues lead nowhere and it is discovered that science has been on the wrong path, then science will self correct. Attempting to generate unfounded fear is counterproductive.

Psychiatry, Eugenics and Mad in America Scare Tactics – Part II

By Dr David Laing Dawson

I am not shocked that we passed through a phase in our evolving civilization when we seriously considered Eugenics. Until we understood a little about genes and inherited traits, every serious abnormality must have been considered an accident or an act of God, perhaps a punishment for some immoral thought or deed. Certainly a stigma and something for a family to hide, if it could. And, at the time, the tribe or village would feel no collective responsibility to look after the impaired child, the disabled adult. This infant and child would be a burden on the family alone until she died, usually very young.

But coinciding with a time our tribes, our villages, our city-states, and then our countries developed a social conscience, a new social contract, and accepted the collective burden to care for these disabled members, we began to learn of their genetic origins. It would be entirely logical to then consider the possibility of prevention.

When medicine discovers a good thing, it always takes it too far, and then pulls back. When men and institutions have power we always, or some of us at least, abuse it, until we put in some safeguards. And there is always at least one psychopathic charismatic leader lurking nearby willing to bend both science and pseudo science to his own purposes.

But we have, here in the western world, passed through those phases (and hope to not repeat them). Now every year we find genetics is more complicated, that there are more factors involved. And every year we pinpoint at least one more detectable genetic arrangement (combinations, additions, deletions, modifiers, absences) that cause specific and serious abnormalities.

But here is where we are now medically and socially in the Western World: We can test the parents' genetic makeup, we can test the amniotic fluid, if indicated we can test the fetal cells, we can offer parents a choice to abort or not; we can tell them of projected difficulties, available treatment or lack thereof, likely outcome, and possible future improvements in treatment and cure. We have also socially evolved sufficiently (and are rich enough) for the state to assume some, or, if necessary, all of the burden of care.

That is where we are, notwithstanding the difficulties of providing this care, and the antiabortion crowd: Some genetic certainties, some intrauterine tests, some blood tests for carriers, some absolute and some statistical predictions, and parental choice.

Now we come to genetics and mental illness. We have no certainties; we have some statistics; we have no intrauterine tests, no blood tests, and we have parental choice.

For science to not continue to pursue a genetic line of inquiry for serious mental illness would be a travesty.

Nature/Nurture. I think I entered psychiatry at the height of this academic debate. On one hand the psychoanalysts dominated US psychiatry, while biological psychiatry (Kraepelian psychiatry) dominated British psychiatry. (R.D. Laing was an outlier). Meanwhile psychology figured if you could train a dog to salivate at a bell you could train any kid to do anything. At the same time many poets, essayists, and not a few Marxist sociologists were telling us that the insane were not insane. It was the world around them that was insane. From Biological Determinism to parental cause to the Tabula Rasa and back to Social Determinism.

Other psychiatrists worked hard to find a way of including all possible factors: the bio/psycho/social model. (Which I would like to see redefined as the bio/socio/psychological model, for it is clear to me that our behaviors are driven first by our biology, secondly by our social nature, by social imperatives, and thirdly by our actual psychology, our cognitive processes. (Just watch Donald Trump)

How much of our nature is determined genetically, or epigenetically in the womb, and how much by our experiences as infants and children and teens and adults? When it comes to human behavior it is clearly all of the above, to different degrees and proportions.

The studies show that the risk of developing schizophrenia is 50% if your identical twin has schizophrenia, whether raised together or apart. This was often touted to show that 50% of the causative factors for schizophrenia must be environmental. But we now know that identical twins are **not really genetically identical**. And the interplay of genes, genome, brain development and environment is time sensitive. (Despite her fluent English my wife still stumbles on some English sounds. They were just not the sounds her brain was hearing at age 3.)

On the other hand identical twins reared apart are later found to have developed surprisingly similar traits, speech patterns, skills, and interests. And on every visit with my daughter in Australia she complains about the knees I bequeathed her.

As I mentioned before, genetics gets more complicated the more we are able to study it. Some DNA sequences seem to predict a mental illness in adolescence or adulthood but not the exact one.

Of course that finding may reflect not so much on environmental influences as on the vagaries of our definitions, our current diagnostic system.

An old colleague once remarked that our criteria for the diagnosis of schizophrenia are at the stage of the diagnosis of Dropsy in about 1880. I think he exaggerated. They are closer today to a diagnosis of Pneumonia in 1940. (Note that we can now distinguish a pneumonia that is bacterial caused, from viral, or autoimmune, or inhalational, and which bacteria, but our antibiotics help only one form of pneumonia, and each of these forms of pneumonia may have one of numerous underlying problems (biological and social) causing the vulnerability to developing pneumonia.)

For mental illness the development of drugs (1960's on) **that actually work much of the time** threw a monkey wrench into this ongoing debate and inquiry. It tipped the balance to biological thinking for many of us. But it is a logical fallacy to assume a treatment that works reveals the original cause. The treatment is disrupting the chain of pathogenesis at some point but not necessarily at the origin of the chain.

We will continue to argue nature/nurture, and science will continue to investigate. And doctors will continue to treat with the best tools they have available.

If Dr. Berezin is correct (which he is not) and serious mental illnesses like schizophrenia, manic depressive illness, autism, and debilitating depression, OCD, and anxiety are all caused by "trauma", much hope is lost and we will not find good treatments and cures for centuries. For today, despite what Donald Trump and Fox News tell us, in our childhoods in Europe and North America we **experience far less** trauma, strife, deprivation and loss than every generation before us. Yet mental illness persists in surprisingly persistent numbers.

Dr. Berezin is taking a leaf from the Donald J Trump book. He is trying to frighten you with images of violence, abuse, regression, lawlessness for his own purposes. He is waving Eugenics and Hitler at you in much the same way Donald conjures images of rapists, criminals, illegals, and terrorists streaming across the American border.

But lets get real:

Serious mental illness (schizophrenia, manic depressive illness, debilitating anxiety and OCD, true medical, clinical depression) are little helped with non-pharmacological treatments alone. The reason we do not see today, mute and stuporous men and women lying in hospital beds refusing to eat and wasting away is because we have the pharmacological means (and ECT) to treat depression. The reason we do not have four Queen Victorias and six Christs residing in every hospital is because we now have drugs that control Psychotic Illness. The reason we don't see thin elated starving naked men standing on hills screaming at the moon until they die of exhaustion is because we now have drugs that control mania. The reason we don't have as many eccentrics living in squalor collecting their own finger nail clippings and urine is because we now have very effective pharmacology to treat serious OCD.

All of these people also need social help and someone in their corner, but without the actual pharmacological treatment it will get us nowhere.

(Though, I must admit, today, you may be able to see untreated catatonia, untreated stuporous and agitated depression, untreated mania and untreated schizophrenia in some of our correctional facilities).

But lets look at the less serious mental problems as well for a minute. A patient tells me she is afraid of flying, and always avoided it. But her father is dying in another province and she needs to fly there to see him one last time. She is terrified of getting on that plane. She imagines having a panic attack and disrupting the flight.

A fear of flying. A phobia of flying. Those of us who have such a phobia can usually manage by avoiding travel by plane.

But my patient. She needs to make this trip. Now perhaps I should send her to a trauma therapist who might uncover the fact a school friend was lost over Lockerbie and have her grieve about this, and still be afraid of flying; or perhaps to a cognitive behavioural therapist who might try to convince her that her fears are unfounded, pointing out how air travel is safer than car travel; or perhaps a desensitization approach in which the counselor uses relaxation techniques and has her imagine being at the airport, boarding the plane, and perhaps accompanying her to the airport on the day of travel; or perhaps I should find out if the fear is based on sitting so close to 300 strangers for 5 hours, or riding in a 20 ton contraption at the speed of sound two miles in the air; or spending 5 hours locked in a cigar shaped coffin with 300 strangers.....

Or I might simply prescribe for her five dollars worth of Lorazepam and offer a few encouraging words to get her through the trip.

Then lets look at something in between, like ADHD, one of the diagnoses mentioned by Dr. Berezin.

It is not a difficult equation for me. The child can't sit still in class, he is too easily distracted, lacks focus, can't concentrate, always being reprimanded by the teacher, socially ostracized because he intrudes, he pokes, he speaks out of turn, he angers too easily.

To become a successful adult he **needs to succeed in at least one thing**, if not more than one thing, in his childhood. If, with accommodation at school, and some parental strategies, some adaptational strategies, such as being allowed to wear earphones and take an exercise break every 20 minutes, have one-on-one instruction, good diet, better sleep – if these work, then he may not need medication.

If they don't work it means he will fail socially and academically and maybe at home as well. He will be in trouble all the time. He will become surly, or give up, or become more aggressive, or depressed. In his teens he will self-medicate.

If the difference between a child failing or succeeding socially and academically is a single pill taken with breakfast it would be, to use

that word again, a travesty to not prescribe that pill. And that is true whether the ultimate or necessary causative factor is inherited or acquired, or some complex combination of biological vulnerability, epigenetics, infantile and toddler experience, parenting styles, pedagogic methods, diet, and video game addiction.

On Naturopathy and Psychiatry

By Dr David Laing Dawson

Naturopathy, Homeopathy

I am growing intolerant.

Many of my patients over the years have attended Naturopaths. And I assume that for every 10 who confess this, the number must be closer to 20 or 30 for the 10 usually confess with a sheepish grin. I seldom react save for a slight smile and nod for it is usually a harmless event and most Naturopaths, I am pretty sure, do not recommend that their patients stop actual medical treatment.

One mother came back with the story that the Naturopath had studied the blood of her three sons under a microscope and found all three samples revealed high concentrations of parasites. I began to react but first asked what she had recommended. A good diet and lots of exercise was the prescription, so I let it pass. How long would it take to explain that if, indeed, her children did have parasites in their blood we should be heading to the emergency of the nearest hospital as quickly as possible.

Another told me his Naturopath had put him on Lithium. Now, if that were true I should monitor his serum lithium levels, his kidney and thyroid function. But I didn't. Because I assumed if there was some actual lithium in the concoction he was given it was miniscule, less than might be found in a pistachio nut, or, in fact, embodied that other silliness of naturopathy and homeopathy: some distilled or diluted water that had fond memories of a lithium salt that once resided in it.

So naturopathy and homeopathy are mostly harmless. And it was a logical approach to some dis-ease in the early 19th century, based then on two extrapolations: 1. We thought a few dis-eases might be caused by deficiencies in diets so perhaps all dis-eases are caused by deficiencies. 2. We had no idea what those deficiencies might be so let us give each patient a concoction comprised of small amounts of many things and let his or her body choose which it needs. Not a bad idea at the time. Especially at a time when barber-surgeons and physicians were experimenting with drugs and procedures that could do more harm than good.

But we are no longer in the 19th century, and we know a little more about human and animal physiology now. And we can test for deficiencies if they are suspected. And we now know those deficiencies can occur from an absence in diet, or a genetic or acquired inability to absorb and use a particular vitamin, protein, amino acid, or mineral. And we know that a true deficiency leads to a specific clinical condition.

I forced myself to read an "award-winning" article by Jonathan E. Prousky from the Townsend Letter which purports to be the Examiner of alternative medicine. He starts by presenting two cases (fictional compilations he admits), and then proceeds to slander most medical care and all psychiatric care (with the exception of brief interventions for psychosis). In fact he lists psychiatric treatment and the "mental health system" as "oppressors causing a negative load on the allostatic system". (meaning they are bad for you)

But then he goes on to list the alternatives that will make you well again and keep you well. They are:

- Exercise
- Good diet
- Connecting with Nature (a walk in the woods)
- Limiting computer/TV/video gaming time.
- Religious involvement, or at least paying attention to this
- Regular adequate sleep
- And finally, supplements of vitamins and Omega 3

My mother would have agreed in the mid 20th century. Though she insisted on fruit and vegetables for Vit C and A, meat and beans for the B vitamins and iron, milk for calcium, playing outside for Vitamin D, a little extra D through the winter, and Cod Liver Oil for brain development. She would also talk of balance, a good nights sleep, and moderation in all things.

We medical doctors spend a lot of time reviewing exercise, diet, finding a balance in life, limiting gaming and virtual reality, seeking comfort and solace in nature (or vacations, dancing, music, art, work, hobbies, relationships, helping others) finding a way of accepting the realities of life and living with the unknowns, getting a good night's sleep, eating breakfast, and taking Vit D and Omega 3.

All good advice providing that we don't overdose on vitamin supplements, for excessive quantities can do damage.

But not as a replacement for medical or psychiatric treatment for illness. Not as a replacement for vaccination. Not as a replacement for real blood tests, scans, medical examinations and investigations, treatment with antibiotics, treatment with modern medicines, medical treatment for depression, severe anxiety, schizophrenia, bipolar illness. Not as a replacement or "alternative" for science.

The nonsense of naturopathy and homeopathy is not harmless when it convinces people to ignore or forgo real medical prevention and treatment for themselves and their children.

On Mental Illness – Let's Not Wring Our Hands But Actually Do Something

By Dr David Laing Dawson

The last few days, thanks to our local newspaper and the television, I have been bombarded with mental health news. This could be a good thing. Heightened awareness, increased sensitivity, decreased stigma, having a public conversation about it, making politicians and lawmakers aware.

But it has almost all been over-inclusive wringing of hands, bemoaning the state of the nation, the suicidality of our youth, the stresses of modern life, the bad behavior and instability of our classrooms, the internet vulnerability of our children, the dramatically increased use of marijuana which is now, they say, ten times more powerful than the stuff we toked in the 60's while singing "Puff the Magic Dragon."

As is so often the case these days the words and phrases "mental health", "mental health issues", "addictions", "behavioural issues", "stress", "anxiety", "mental illness", "addiction issues", are used interchangeably.

The most egregious of these misnomers often comes in the form of "He is known to suffer from mental health."

Am I too concerned with semantics here? I don't think so. Because I think all this fraught hand wringing, vague euphemisms, contradictory word usage, broad generalizations, and statistically implied causal relationships can only lead to two kinds of unhelpful responses:

1. The news itself, defined so broadly, so all inclusively, so vaguely, and with such a sense of urgency, becomes just another stress to bear.
2. Money is found, a program is announced, some general response that will allow the politicians to appear to be doing something to "solve the problem" and boast in the legislature or town council, while knowing it will do nothing to help specific individuals

who actually suffer from specific mental illnesses.

At least response number two will help alleviate the damage of response number one. But response number two is all too often some general manipulation of optics, some appearance of action to "eliminate crime", or to provide a telephone number to call for those who are stressed or "experiencing suicidal thoughts."

Okay. There are social, political, and economic factors that contribute to mental illness and disability. And we could and should gradually ameliorate these through social and political programs that reduce poverty (minimum wage, disability pension, and social assistance increases), increase the availability of affordable housing, make day care more affordable and accessible, ensure we have an educated population, help youth transition from childhood to full independence (support, training, internships, money management programs), stop sending young men and women to war and trauma, ensure some of the profits from alcohol and gambling go to alleviate the damage done by alcohol and gambling, fund and **evaluate** specific targeted programs to reduce the social cost of addictions, and to counter the misogynist messages our young men are now acquiring through social media, pervasively available pornography, and hateful song lyrics.

But there are a number of specifically identifiable and specifically treatable mental illnesses that we could target in a far more specific and effective way. These are:

Anxiety Disorder
Obsessive Compulsive Disorder
Depression
Bi-Polar Disorder
Schizophrenia.

These specific disorders (not withstanding the researchers' and clinicians' ongoing search for more clarity, specificity, and causality) can be very specific causes of disability, distress, failure, and suicide.

But we can identify them; we have the tools to detect them; and we have the tools to treat them. And doing this, providing funds and creating programs to do this, would be far more effective than hand wringing.

Take suicide for instance. There are a large number of social factors (loss, divorce, alcoholism, poverty, unemployment, debilitating illness, aging, trauma) that increase the risk of suicide. Some of these we can do nothing about. We can chip away at others through legislation and social programs.

But there are some specific causes of suicide (actual suicide, not threats and thoughts) for which we do have the tools to detect, intervene, and treat. And these are the mental illnesses listed above.

(I think I must point out here that the proliferation of hot lines, crisis lines, help lines, phone numbers to call over the past twenty years, has **NOT** changed the actual completed suicide rate in any jurisdiction I know of. But there have been studies demonstrating that helping and teaching family doctors in the detection and treatment of **depression** has lowered the rate of actual suicide.)

So what we should focus on are specific programs for early detection and comprehensive treatment of the mental illnesses listed above. Or better targeted funding for the services that do that now, and the linkages between them. These linkages are crucial in order to move from suspicion, to detection, through assessment, to expert treatment: Parent and teacher to counselor and social worker to family doctor and pediatrician to mental health program with psychologists and psychiatrists.

Editor's Note Dr David Laing Dawson has been practicing psychiatry for many years. He is a former professor of psychiatry in the Faculty of Health Sciences at McMaster University in Hamilton, ON and the former chief of psychiatry at the Hamilton Psychiatric Hospital. He is the author of *Schizophrenia in Focus, Relationship Management of the Borderline Patient and The Adolescent Owner's Manual. He has also written and directed a number of films on mental illness.*

Psychotropic Medication, Addiction, Withdrawal, Discontinuation, Relapse

By Dr David Laing Dawson

I can offer some thoughts on this from many years of observation.

Addiction is addiction. Defined as the development of tolerance (requiring more and more of the drug for the same effect) and physiological withdrawal symptoms upon stopping the drug.

Benzodiazepine drugs are addictive. The "pam" drugs. They are safest prescribed for short periods or for intermittent use. But most of us struggle with this because they offer instant relief and there are few alternatives. (this deserves a longer discussion at another time)

SSRI and NSRI antidepressant medications are not (by definition) addictive. We do not develop tolerance and require higher and higher doses. But when they are stopped abruptly patients often suffer "discontinuation" symptoms. Perhaps this is a euphemism for withdrawal symptoms but usually they are not severe, and some people come off SSRI medication without any such symptoms at all.

Usually these symptoms are unlike a true relapse and are short lived. They are described many ways by people using such words and phrases as "not like myself, foggy headed, pinging, buzzing or electric shocks in my head".

Some of the SSRI and NSRI medications have worse discontinuation symptoms than others. Perhaps Paxil and Effexor XR are the worst offenders. But again, some patients go on and off these medications without any ill effects. Strategies to ameliorate withdrawal effects include very very slow weaning and switching to an SSRI with a longer half-life.

And it is usually not difficult to distinguish these withdrawal symptoms from a relapse of the original illness being treated with these drugs. The withdrawal symptoms are almost immediate, depending on the half-life of the medication; they are odd feelings rather than the slow return of the depression or anxiety disorder they were treating.

A true relapse of the illness may occur months or even years after discontinuation. And usually the discontinuation symptoms last a few days to a couple of weeks. When these illnesses relapse (depression, anxiety, OCD) the symptoms are usually identical to those of the first episode. This fact is one of the reasons it is reasonable to call Depression, Anxiety, and OCD illnesses.

Anxiety disorders and depressions can be chronic persistent disorders or relapsing and remitting disorders. They can be seasonal or more closely associated with events and transitions in life.

Usually these medications work. And the more severe the illness the more dramatically effective they can be.

Do these drugs actually cause a later vulnerability to depression? I think the short answer is "no". Impossible to prove of course but I have not seen it. But I have seen much relief from suffering and dramatic improvement in function.

With all that, the SSRI's are undoubtedly over prescribed for less serious mood problems, unhappiness, and disappointment.

Of course **if** non-pharmacological means of alleviating mood problems do so for you on their own, then by all means use these instead: exercise, meditation, yoga, SADS lamp, counseling and therapies of any kind, better diet and sleep, better balance in life……

But I must admit that in 40 plus years of prescribing life-balance, exercise, meditation and yoga, my patient compliance rate is running roughly 5 percent. It is very hard to initiate any of these activities if you are house bound with anxiety or morbidly depressed.

Anti-Psychiatry

By Marvin Ross

I really don't get it – anti-psychiatry that is. I can understand that if someone has had a bad experience with a psychiatrist, they might be wary and hostile. After all, not all doctors are good and I have no doubt that most of us have run into a bad one over the course of our lives. I certainly have seen my share of rude, arrogant and stupid doctors from family practitioners to cardiologists but I do not condemn them all. I do not devote my energy to attacking emergency medicine because of a bad ER doc I've encountered.

A lot of the anti-psychiatrists I've encountered fall into this category. They've had a bad experience and generalize to all. But a lot of the others aren't in this group. They are people who have decided that their time should be devoted to attacking psychiatry as their contribution to freedom of the individual or to the good of mankind. And, for the most part, they know very little of neuroscience, medicine or mental illness. If they truly want to make a difference, they should devote their time to advocating for better care and treatment for the seriously mentally ill or to help with the growing problem of refugees, world peace, homelessness, child poverty, and the list goes on.

For the most part, they are mistaken in their views of psychiatry as Mark Roseman pointed out so brilliantly in his review Deconstructing Psychiatry. I highly recommend that people read that. His analysis is far more detailed than mine but I would like to comment on a few of the common myths that he covers in more detail.

The one complaint that is common among the anti-psychiatry mob is that psychiatrists are controlling people who give an instant diagnosis and then force their patients to take toxic drugs.

People do not go to see psychiatrists by calling one up or walking into their offices. They need to be referred by a general practitioner or via a hospital like an emergency room. And they would only be referred to a psychiatrist if they had psychiatric problems that were beyond the expertise of the general practitioner. That referral would only be made after the general practitioner had ruled out non-psychiatric causes of the symptoms and behaviour.

Like all doctors, the psychiatrist will take a detailed history from the patient, consider possible diagnoses and recommend appropriate treatment. The treatment recommended is based on the professional guidelines outlining evidence based strategies. These are the practice guidelines used by the American Psychiatric Association. Similar guidelines are used in different countries. The cornerstones of any medical practice are to do no harm and to relieve suffering.

I often hear comments and criticisms that a psychiatrist put someone on toxic drugs that they were then forced to take for eternity. A comment to my blog on the anti-psychiatry scholarship at the University of Toronto stated "based on the results of a positive diagnosis (from a 15 minute questionnaire score) a patient (including young children) may receive powerful psychoactive drugs for years, the long term effects of which are not yet known."

As I said above, the diagnosis is not based on a 15 minute questionnaire but on an extensive evaluation. And, regardless of the medical area, drugs are always (or should be) prescribed in the lowest dose for a short period of time and the patient brought back in for evaluation of efficacy and side effects. The goal is to find the lowest dose that is effective with minimal side effects. This is a process called drug titration.

If the drug is not effective or if it causes too many unwanted side effects, it will be changed. No one is forced to take a drug that does them little good in any discipline of medicine. Surely, the patient does have choice to continue with that doctor or not and to take the advice that is offered. People who see psychiatrists are not held captive.

When it comes to children, they are not seen in isolation as the anti-psych criticism I quoted above implied. They are seen with their families who, understandably, do not want their kids on powerful drugs. There are long discussions with the psychiatrist where all less invasive means are explored. When pharmaceuticals are prescribed, the parents are at complete liberty to stop them if they do not work or if they cause troublesome side effects. The children are not held captive by the psychiatrist and force fed pills against the wishes of the parents.

When a child does continue to take the medication it is because it is having a benefit and there are no troublesome side effects. I remember a mother who resisted Ritalin for her hyperactive child for years telling me how well it worked once she decided to give it a try. "I wish I had tried it much earlier", she told me. "It would have saved so much grief."

The anti-psychiatry bunch also assert that mental illnesses do not exist and cite the lack of any one definitive test to prove bipolar disorder, schizophrenia or other afflictions. Quite true but the same can be said for many other maladies. How about Parkinson's as but one example. Doctors cannot measure the amount of dopamine in the brain (which is depleted in Parkinson's) to definitively say that the person has the condition. They determine the presence of this condition based upon observing the person and his or her movements.

Alzheimer's is another. Like with schizophrenia, it is diagnosed by eliminating all possible other reasons for the observed dementia and when none can be found, the diagnosis of Alzheimer's is made. On autopsy, there will be found specific markers but no one ever gets an autopsy to prove that the doctor was correct. And rarely is anyone with schizophrenia autopsied on death but this is a lengthy list of the abnormalities that demonstrate that it is a disorder of the brain.

The anti-psychiatry group should be looked upon with the same disdain that sensible people look upon the anti-vax faction.

Anti-Psychiatry Bold and Profane

By Dr David Laing Dawson

Let me make a simple bold and somewhat profane statement about anti-psychiatry. Which I take to mean, really, anti-medical-pharmaceutical-psychiatry.

When I entered medical school and later psychiatry, I would have been content to believe that all these psychiatric illnesses were entirely "psychological" in origin and form. It was the 1960's so I was even quite ready to believe that all this insanity was really a sane response to an insane world.

Insanity is fascinating. I have spent hours talking with, listening to people who believe the CIA is watching them, their phones are bugged, the television sends them messages, they are emissaries of God, the voices tell them they must kill someone, they are controlled by radar, Xrays, Radio waves, microchips, which in turn are controlled by the police, shadowy evil figures, particular races, the CIA, the Mafia, Martians and Venusians. The devil has figured in many of these conversations. God in many others.

I have talked with people who fear to leave the house, who keep the blinds down lest the watchers watch them, people who can't cross an open patch of land, people who must count the ceiling tiles, who must pray every time they think a bad thought, people who must have every sequence of action and thought end in an even number.

I have talked with people too depressed to talk, to move, to shit, to piss. I have talked with people too agitated, too distraught, too full of dread to sit. I have talked to people who assumed I came from either God or The Devil or both or either. I have talked to people who could not complete a single sentence without it wandering elsewhere. I have written questions on paper for people who feared to talk at all. I have talked with people who keep their eyes on the door, or on the ground.

I write fiction and plays. Dreaming up historic, family, life event, and even intrauterine causes for mental illness is fascinating. I have entered a patient's delusions. I have explained to a woman who thought her self to be Queen that I was the Prime Minister and therefore, in our parliamentary democracy, someone she could listen to. I have talked to "the illegitimate son of Adolf Hitler", to a man who could "whistle up the wind", and to women who set themselves on fire. I have talked with a man who killed two children and then their mother.

I would actually be content (but for the suffering from depression of my own mother) to have these people in humane mental hospitals, fed and clothed and active and cared for and available for me to talk with, explore, dialogue with, interpret, help to find a psychological cause, a trauma, a series of adverse childhood experiences that might explain their perceptions of reality. In fact I have done all of these. I have sat next to a manic with arm on her chair to comfort without touching, on a mattress on the floor with a man wanting to kill somebody, in parking lots and back porches. I have talked with a "King of Kings."

It is fascinating. It is human. It is dramatic. It is sometimes comedic. It can provide me with wonderful fodder for my fiction, my plays.

But I am also a doctor. And as much as I romantically like the idea of being an Alienist, living in the manor house of the large Asylum and dining with the "lunatics", or setting them free to roam a Grecian Isle, I must try my best to relieve their suffering. And, it seems, that from the mid 1960's, just when I entered this field of psychiatry, we began to develop pharmaceutical agents that actually work, that relieve suffering, that restore functioning, that control these terrible illnesses.

My patients want their suffering relieved. They want their function restored. They want their illnesses controlled.

So, my anti-psychiatry friends, I must continue to prescribe drugs, relieve suffering, help restore functioning, and forgo the psychoanalytic pleasures, the philosophical, poetic explorations, the mad interpretations, just as I must insist on vaccinations for all children, and forgo all the wonderful and fanciful spiritual and moral interpretations of spots, and fevers, and delirium of the early 19th century.

d morally, and kindly, pray before bedtime, and avoid certain pleasurable but dangerous substances, we can also avoid dis-ease, illness, and a fall from grace.

We know that alcoholism and addiction include an action taken, engaged in, by the sufferer, engaged in willfully, of free will, and that

recovery from addiction will entail a mind set, a decision, a commitment, a major effort on the part of the sufferer. So with alcohol and addiction programs this process is supported, encouraged, often through peer support, non-judgmental encouragement, soul searching, an acknowledgement of weakness, a trust in a "higher power", and even, in some programs, forms of confession and penance. When we talk of treatment for alcoholism and addictions we are really using the word "treatment" to mean a complex sophisticated form of persuasion. We don't really have a treatment for those two problems beyond persuasion and support.

In the post WW II era, our mental hospitals became "psychiatric hospitals", and, a few years later, at least one ward in most general hospitals became a psychiatric ward, or colloquially, a "psyche ward". This naming was important. It acknowledged a medical specialty, and a group of diseases treated by that specialty, much like an orthopedic department, a gynecology wing, a surgery ward. In fact the federal funding in Canada to support general hospital psychiatry wards (via federal provincial transfer payments) was a considered effort to acknowledge mental illness as illness, deserving of the same attitudes, funding, and professional support as "physical" illnesses.

Through the 1970's and 80's it appeared to be working. Programs were developed, new more effective medications were developed, attitudes were changing, physical facilities were improved, and maybe, we thought, this de-institutionalization will work.

Mind you, addictions got short shrift from the mental health system in those years (though the hospitals were psychiatric hospitals, the overall system of care was still called "the mental health system"). Generally addicts and alcoholics were told that they would have to get those problems attended to before we could help them with their mental illnesses. They had to first attend detoxification programs and then alcohol and addiction programs, which often had little patience for either mental illness or psychiatric treatment.

So detox centers, alcohol and addiction treatment programs developed apart from and separate from psychiatric wards and hospitals. And from these centers the "recovery model" developed. The word alone is nothing but positive, but it contains all the implications and expectations and attitudes outlined four paragraphs above. It implies that full recovery is possible***, if you put in the effort***. Peer support, will power, the power of positive thinking, goal setting, avoiding negative thinking, take life a day at a time, take responsibility for yourself........

And, absolutely, for addictions and alcoholism, recovery can be defined as a life free of alcohol and drugs, and it is certainly achievable.

And through all this, our folk wisdom, that wisdom that often governs legislation and attitude, maintained a conviction that, ultimately, alcoholism and addictions are the sufferer's responsibility. If he does not get well, or clean and sober, he is culpable, or at least, ultimately, to some degree, the architect of his own fate. And folk wisdom was shifting to believe that this is not true for schizophrenia, manic-depressive illness, depression or anxiety disorder. These are illnesses requiring treatment. They are usually chronic illnesses. Full and complete recovery is rare, though medications can alleviate symptoms and prevent relapse. There is nothing the sufferer can do **on his own** to prevent or stop these illnesses. And for these illnesses we do have actual treatment.

And then.... actually I'm not sure how this happened.... but somehow the bureaucrats and perhaps a few idealists, managed to bring these two systems under one much more economical roof. Three words were lost in this recent transition: "psychiatric", "illness", and "hospital".

And suddenly we now have a multitude of "Centers for Addiction and Mental Health".

And while this undoubtedly saves money, and perhaps serves better those who suffer both addictions and mental illness, it has had, in my opinion, some very negative unintended consequences.

1. The recovery model, well suited to addictions, has been foisted upon those suffering from mental illness.
2. The stigma of mental illness has been entrenched by the use of the paradoxical euphemism "mental health".
3. We have inadvertently allowed the folk wisdom of acknowledging personal responsibility for addictions (blame) to rub off on those suffering from diseases of the brain, those suffering from schizophrenia and manic-depressive illness.
4. *And ultimately it has allowed us well-meaning citizens to feel*

comfortable that now, not in 1950 or 1960 or 1970, but now, in 2014, our jails and prisons are filled with the seriously mentally ill.

Journalists, Medical Research and Medical Practice

By Marvin Ross and Dr David Laing Dawson

As a medical writer and as someone who works in the daily trenches of serious mental illness in my own family, I find people like Robert Whitaker dangerous. For those who aren't familiar with him, he is a medical journalist from Boston who is highly critical of the long term use of medication for schizophrenia even though he is neither a scientific researcher nor clinician.

My earlier criticisms of his work appeared in the Huffington Post as Journalists are not medical experts and Leave the schizophrenia diagnosis to the experts please.

One of Whitaker's key criticisms is that the long term use of antipsychotics in the treatment of schizophrenia makes people worse not better. A group of researchers in New York set out to see if they could replicate what they called his "troubling interpretation" and published their results in a recent issue of the American Journal of Orthopsychiatry.

Their hypothesis was what Whitaker contended that the long term use of antipsychotics resulted in worse outcomes than people who are not treated. They wondered if a systematic appraisal of all the literature would produce the same results as claimed by Whitaker. They looked at 18 studies which included the four that Whitaker used. They pointed out that Whitaker used an additional 6 studies to come to his conclusion but they did not include them because they were review articles that did not report separated data on the exposure groups or were ecological studies which did not report on individual level data.

Of the 18 studies they looked at, only 3 supported the hypothesis that long term treatment with medication causes harm to patients. 8 studies found the opposite and 7 were mixed. These researchers, however, also did not find that long term treatment resulted in greater benefits than harm which is, frankly, not surprising. Some recent studies show that some people with schizophrenia can manage well without long term drug use which Whitaker likes to cite. But there is also no way to predict who can actually achieve that. That is a caveat in all those studies and a fact that Whitaker seems to ignore. (see my post on leave the diagnosis to experts).

Lumping all people with schizophrenia together for a study is bound to have problems since schizophrenia is very likely more than one disease. When Bleuler first coined the term schizophrenia in 1908, he called it the schizophrenias to indicate that it was more like a spectrum than a single entity. Unfortunately, science has not reached the point where the different forms can be identified. An editorial in the January 1, 2016 issue of the American Journal of Psychiatry makes that very point. Current treatment algorithms, it says, do not take into account the substantial interindividual variability in response to antipsychotic drugs.

And, a recent study of first episode patients published in the Journal of Clinical Psychiatry found a greater relapse for those who went off medication after they were stabilized. Decisions to try to reduce doses and to go off are best left to the individual patients working with their psychiatrist. Going off or staying on medication is described by my blogging colleague Dr Dawson who has close to 50 years clinical experience treating patients in a variety of situations. Here is what he has to say:

We doctors over treat at times and under treat at other times. And occasionally we get it just right.

Studies show that family doctors are much more likely to under treat than over treat (pain, depression, arthritis), with specialists erring in the other direction. This is as one would expect, for specialists receive their patients after a family doctor has deemed the case too complex, too resistant to a first line of treatment, or simply beyond her zone of knowledge, skill and comfort.

I have been guilty of both under treating and over treating, probably more often the former. These are type 1 and type 2 errors. If we work to totally eliminate one type of error we will increase the incidence of the other.

We need to be vigilant catching both types of error and correct or ask for help, without letting our egos get in the way.

My patient tells me she is feeling much better now that she has stopped taking those pills I prescribed for her. And at that moment I must allow my feeling of relief and pleasure seeing her look and sound better over-ride this small insult to my ego. Unless I know for sure this is a relapsing illness that will re-emerge within a few weeks, perhaps worse than before.

I also know that it may take a relapse or two or three before we are both sure it is better to suffer the minor discomforts caused by these pharmaceutical agents than the blackness of severe depression, the torture of obsessions, the horrors of psychosis, or the social destruction of mania.

It is really a very small percentage of people who have suffered these severe illnesses who would willingly give up the medication that treats and prevents them. I am usually the one to suggest it may be time for a cautious reduction.

And those that quit them and return to a state of depression, obsession, psychosis, or mania do so for a variety of reasons. Occasionally the side effects were much too severe, or the drug was not helping much. The financial cost too much to bear. The very fact of needing these medications to keep sane can be, for some, an intolerable thought. A manic may remember the ecstasy and not the night in a jail cell, for which he can blame others. Another may find that the drugs he can buy on the street give him, at least temporarily, total relief. Still another may quit simply because there is no one near to remind him, to support him, occasionally to insist. And then a few who prefer to believe their true nature consists of special powers, a supreme intelligence, a grand future, clear reason to be, to be loved by a movie star, to be a hero, to have a unique relationship with God, to have a clear and present or distant antagonist – who prefer to live with this sense of self no matter the earthly consequences – which can always be explained away – than to accept the earth-bound but often meager existence provided by faithfully taking one's medication.

But most people, when sane, prefer to remain sane, even if it means a dry mouth, a little dizziness upon arising too quickly, blood tests more frequently, a harder time keeping weight under control.

As one patient recently said to me: "Thank God for these big pharmaceutical companies."

To which I responded, "Not everyone would share that sentiment."

And he then said, "Why not? Without them you and I would be having this conversation in the asylum."

Madness and Meaning

By Dr David Laing Dawson

As a young physician entering the world of the asylum, the mental hospital, the world of insanity, like many others before and since, I was fascinated by the prospect of finding meaning within madness, understanding behaviours that appeared, at first blush, inexplicable, understanding the de-contextualized speech patterns of many patients, understanding their delusions and voices.

This was the era of Timothy Leary, of a wish on the part of some to find a chemical path to enlightenment, the era of R.D. Laing seeking parental and family causes of insanity, of Thomas Szasz telling us that mental illness is a myth, the time of Foucault telling us that our society causes madness, and Alan Watts telling us that, really, madness was just an alternate flight path.

And, I must admit, madness, delusions, hallucinations, voices, fractured speech patterns, catatonia, mania, and even stuporous depression, contain rich and fertile ground for an artistic and literary imagination, and always fodder for philosophical questions about reality, meaning, semiotics, the nature of a human being, the manner in which we define deviance.

In our therapeutic communities of the day we talked and talked, in small groups and large groups. We listened to delusional ranting, to the reporting of voices emanating from the back of the head or from the dead, from an alien spacecraft, from God, and from the devil. I have spoken with several Queens, a few Christs, a man who tried to kill a president, a man harbouring evil beings inside his body, a man with the gift of teleportation, with many who believed the radio and television and popular songs were sending them personal messages, to many who believed they were being controlled by radar, radio waves, microchips, to men who wanted to cut off their genitals, to others who wanted to gouge out their eyes, to a few who wanted to kill someone who was controlling them from afar.

Of course we can find meaning in all of this, in each and every delusion, in each and every ephemeral message. And the meanings can be deep, intellectual, fanciful, alluding to Greek Mythology, Shakespeare, intrusive government programs, Kafka. They can be Freudian, Jungian, Adlerian, Foucaultian. They can even be new age and theosophic.

Or the meaning can be found more simply in those basic parameters of our social world and our sense of self: power, control, influence, intimacy, sexuality, responsibility, worth, love, hate, guilt, fear.

But does this help?

If it helps us empathize, yes. If it helps us form a relationship, develop trust, rapport, acceptance, yes. If it helps us accept these sufferers as fellow human beings, yes.

But might it not be more important to treat that young man who wants to gouge out his eye, before he actually does it, rather than worry about Oedipus Rex?

As For Trauma Causing Schizophrenia: No! No! No!

By Dr David Laing Dawson

Childhood deprivation and childhood trauma, severe and real trauma, can lead to a lifetime of struggle, failure, depression, dysthymia, emotional pain, addictions, alcoholism, fear, emotional dysregulation, failed relationships, an increase in suicide risk, and sometimes a purpose, a mission in life to help others. But not a persistent psychotic illness. On the other hand teenagers developing schizophrenia apart from a protective family are vulnerable, vulnerable to predators and bullies. So we often find a small association between schizophrenia and trauma, but not a causative relationship.

The human brain/mind has a large variety of mechanisms to protect itself when under threat: Avoidance, denial, withdrawal, anger, rage, fainting, fantasy, suppression, repression, derealization, depersonalization, and dissociation. Some of these may appear to be brief psychotic episodes, but they are not the same thing as persistent psychotic illness. In fact, as I have witnessed many times through the past forty years, well meaning therapists who push their patients emotionally, who "dig for underlying traumas and conflicts", who try emotionally-laden or unstructured group therapy with patients who suffer from severe psychotic illness, invariably cause a relapse in the illness. And a relapse in schizophrenia or bipolar illness is not a benign event. This was often justified by the old psychoanalytic dogma "they have to get worse before they can get better." Again no, no, no.

Having a psychotic illness, in itself, and the consequences of that illness, can be traumatic to both the sufferer and his or her family. People with psychotic illness do not need someone probing the wells of their psychic discomfort; they do not need (no matter how well-intended) a therapist scouring their childhood memories in search of an unhealed wound. They need support, safety, security, grounding, and satisfying routine before they can get better. And good medical treatment.

More on Trauma in Youth and Schizophrenia

By David Laing Dawson

This blog is in response to a comment made on an earlier blog called **As For Trauma Causing Schizophrenia: No! No! No!**

The comment was how do you account for this study? And how can you claim that trauma cannot be causative of schizophrenia? https://www.sciencedaily.com/releases/2012/04/120419102440.htm

This is the answer:

There is no doubt severe trauma in childhood can have long lasting effects. But can trauma be a specifically causative element in the development of the full illness schizophrenia? And is it either a necessary causative element or a contributing factor?

Data mining and surveys come up with many associations, some weak, some strong. Fair enough. But we have to examine the definitions of each and every term and understand that association is not necessarily causative. And in this situation we must be very careful what we publicize because any association between trauma and schizophrenia provides support for parent blaming.

I am back to eating butter after something like 20 years of favouring margarine. This because for many years data mining found associations with butter and other animal fats and cardiovascular disease, and only recently further data mining and studies have shown that, au contraire, we need fat, and margarine may be worse than butter. Now I slather butter on my corn and biscuits without guilt. As someone else has pointed out, there is a very strong association between major road accidents and the presence of ambulances.

The word paranoia is used in many of those studies. I don't know how they define it or determine it. Adolescents suffering from anxiety often experience what they call 'paranoia' but we refer to as 'ideas of reference'. They feel their peers are always talking about them, judging them. Some avoid school because of this. Sometimes this feeling becomes a conviction and then it may be prodromal of a psychotic illness.

Bullying is interesting. I have 30 years of experience dealing with families in which a child is reported as being bullied by his peers. There are some distinct subcategories in this: In one subset, when the details are elicited, it turns out the boy in question is as much a perpetrator as a recipient. They taunt one another. But this particular boy tells his mother that Jason called him a "....." in order to get a reaction from his mother, or to avoid something, or simply to get in front of the call that is going to come from Jason's mother or the school.

A second subset is the Asperger/ASD child. They are common targets for bullying, precisely because of the way they react to unfairness, teasing, slights, and taunts. It is not kind and it is not good but they have become targets for bullying precisely because of the social deficits they already exhibit. My own survey reported on this site indicates that at least a third to a half of people diagnosed with schizophrenia have had autistic symptoms since infancy. So I would definitely expect a higher proportion of bullied children to develop a psychotic illness. The bullying is not causative, but the prodromal symptoms of the illness "invite" bullying.

Auditory hallucinations are not, in and of themselves, schizophrenia. People, girls, who have suffered prolonged sexual abuse report a higher incidence of auditory hallucinations. This certainly could be understood as persistent trauma of a particularly disorienting kind causing impairment in the brain's otherwise quite miraculous ability to (usually) locate the locus of a thought or feeling, as well as causing all the other symptoms of PTSD as well.

On the other hand preteen and teen girls with ASD or prodromal symptoms of schizophrenia are vulnerable to predators within a family and neighborhood.

In sum, there are weak associations, though all suffer from our poor definitions and lack of clarity of diagnosis. None are strong enough to be considered causative. And if this were an association between salt intake and hypertension, to publish early causes little harm. (although even here we now have the problem of some people having too little salt in their diet, and other studies showing high salt intake may have nothing to do with hypertension).

But because this **overall weak association** with all its definition and cause/effect problems could support the existing serious prejudice of parent blaming for schizophrenia, I have to stick with my simple, "No. Neither psychological trauma nor poor parenting cause the serious illness we call schizophrenia."

Though, of course, either could make it worse.

Lies, damned lies, and statistics

by David Laing Dawson

Mark Twain said that long before we had computers and a few dozen algorithms we could apply to random numbers to find 'meaningful' patterns.

Data mining and scientific studies that find nothing or negative results seldom get published. So it behooves all academics to find something. To find at least an association that can be inflated by the manner the data is reported. Then it will get published, and the press might even pick it up if it is startling enough.

I am writing this because an article on the front page of our local paper tells us that people who take antidepressants are at risk of premature death. This is based on a local academic's data mining and meta-analysis. The figure quoted is 33% higher risk of premature death and 14% more likelihood of death from cardiovascular disease. They also have to explain away the fact that if you have previous cardiovascular disease the use of antidepressants **does not** increase risk.

First, these are associations, not cause and effect. Secondly the variables are numerous. And the first variable that comes to mind is that the people who take antidepressants probably suffered from anxiety and depression, undoubtedly felt unwell, and did ask their physicians for help. The people who never took antidepressants did not. The only way these figures can be clarified would be to take 10,000 people who attend doctors complaining of anxiety, OCD, and depression and give antidepressants to 5000, and nothing to the other 5000, (randomly selected) and follow over 20 or 30 or 50 years.

Then we have the startling 33%. Well, if 3 people out of 1000 die in one group and 4 in the second group, that is a 33% increase, looking at it one way, but really a **0.1% difference looking at it in a real life way**. These kinds of statistics are often misused in the press. When the actual risk (sorry, not actually RISK, just different finding) of contracting something increases from 1 in a million in one study to 2 in a million in another study that can be reported as a 100% increase.

I am sure antidepressants are both underused and overused. Underused in the rush of clinical practice when severe depression is not recognized or not reported, underused when the person is already self-medicating with marijuana, alcohol or opioids, underused when the dosages used are too small for severe depression – and overused as the go-to-drug for angst and unhappiness.

I am also sure any drug should be avoided if it can be. That goes for anti-hypertensives, statins, antibiotics, and aspirin.

So I did a little data mining of my own. It turns out that the people of **Australia, Iceland, and Sweden** rank in longevity 2, 3, and 4 in the world. Canada and New Zealand follow closely. Japan holds the number one spot but antidepressant data (for interesting cultural reasons) can't be found so I have excluded Japan. On average the people in spots numbers 2,3, and 4 live between 82.4 and 82.8 years. Let's average that to 82.6 years of life expectancy. **Iceland, Australia, and Sweden also rank as the highest antidepressant users,** ranking one, two, and four. (Denmark is number three)

Among the lowest antidepressant users (where data for life expectancy and antidepressant use can be accurately determined) are Estonia, Turkey and Slovakia.The life expectancy for the people of those countries averages 76. **So by simple association we find that the longest lived people in the world consume the greatest number of antidepressant pills per person.**

Applying my own meta analysis to this data I can arrive at the conclusion that high average consumption of antidepressants prolongs (oops, is associated with an increase in) life expectancy by 6.6 years, or almost 9%. The headline this could generate would be: **Prozac increases life expectancy by 9%**

But, academics have an ethical duty to explain the limitations of associations found in population studies and meta-analysis, and the true meaning of various statistical analyses in real life terms.

Reporters should have an ethical duty to avoid golly gee whiz headlines in health matters. (probably in a few other matters as well)

And medical historians should point out the dramatic change in the number of home and hospital beds utilized by moribund patients suffering from severe depression pre 1960 and today.

A curious side note: On the same Google page for Health news there is a report of a British teen dying from “eating her own hair”. They go on to discuss Rapunzel syndrome, and trichophagia. But such a compulsive behaviour is just that. A compulsion. A serious symptom of OCD. And easily treated today with one of those antidepressants maligned in the other article, along with some counseling of course.

In Memory of an Exceptional Advocate

By Marvin Ross

In her life that was cut too short, Dr Carolyn Dobbins has had a tremendous positive influence on those with serious mental illness and their families thanks in part to her book *What A Life Can Be: One Therapist's Take on Schizoaffective Disorder.* Carolyn passed away suddenly at the age of 57 in February at her home in Knoxville, TN

Carolyn had schizoaffective disorder and wrote her book to try to give people a better understanding of that disease. Her book is written in a very unique style as a series of therapy sessions between a therapist and a patient. Initially, she did not want anyone to know that she, herself, had this affliction but I convinced her to "come out of the closet" and she did. By doing so, the impact of what she wrote was much greater.

Carolyn was an alpine skier who could have made the US Olympic team competing at the Lake Placid games had she not become ill. Despite her struggles, she graduated from the University of Utah, did a PhD in psychology at Vanderbilt and worked as a director of an addiction centre in Branson, MO for 12 years and then went into private practice. At one point, she lived in her car during her undergraduate years and was involuntarily committed while doing her PhD. In fact, she was discharged from a mental hospital and then went straight to Vanderbilt to defend her doctoral thesis.

Christina Bruni who writes a blog on serious mental illness and is the author of *Left of the Dial: A Memoir of Schizophrenia*, Recovery, and Hope, did an interview with Carolyn on her blog on Health Central. When she learned of Carolyn's passing, she told me that "She was a true inspiration to many while she was alive".

My own blurb for her work is that it is "A fascinating look into the world of schizoaffective disorder which, at times, is funny, heartbreaking, but above all uplifting. Dr. Carolyn Dobbins describes the onset and progression of this debilitating disease and gives all readers hope."

My own hype was shared by many others. Dr E Fuller Torrey described it as "an inspiration for all who have ever experienced psychosis" and highly recommends it. Dr. Thomas G Burish, a professor of psychology and Provost of Notre Dame said "powerful and revealing, and provides a unique insight into chronic mental disease"

George E Doebler M Div. Special Advisor, Dept. of Pastoral Care, U of Tennessee Medical Center:, Executive Director, emeritus: Association of Mental Health Clergy (now Association of Professional Chaplains) said "It will challenge your thinking about mental illness, about hope, about faith, about who you are."

The review in Library Journal said "people who have been diagnosed with schizoaffective disorders and those close to them will welcome it as an advocacy tool"

Her reviews on Amazon have been incredible. To date, there have been 21 and they are all 5 Star. Carolyn's father tells me that the Barnes and Noble in Knoxville keeps selling out and her book is being used as a text in Psychology at UT Knoxville.

Carolyn was so focused on helping others that she listed her e-mail address in the book so that readers could contact her and many did.

She will be sorely missed but her book is her legacy and it will continue to give help and comfort to those who need it.

Peers are not Medical Professionals

By Marvin Ross

When it comes to people with illnesses helping and providing support for those newly diagnosed with the same illness, I am supportive. It makes perfect sense for people to have a support network of their peers. Many disease groups have some variation of this. When I was involved with the local chapter of the schizophrenia society, there was an excellent buddy program. Family members with newly diagnosed offspring were matched with an experienced family member who could give advice, support and comfort.

It is only in mental illness where lay peer support people are becoming quasi professionals and involved with all aspects of the illness. This, despite the research that shows that their therapeutic role is of little value. The Mental Elf Blog reported on the most recent evaluation of these programs and found that:

"there is currently little evidence to support the clinical effectiveness of this intervention for people with severe mental illness."

So, imagine my surprise to find that there is a social worker from Quebec described as a psychiatric survivor who has developed a program called Gaining Autonomy & Medication Management (GAM) Training for Peer Support Workers. This program was held in Toronto on December 11 but it has been given in a number of other locales throughout North America.

According to a paper written on GAM, "the approach was developed to take into account the many perspectives and relationships that users have with their medication, their knowledge and practices, their experience of mental health workers, and a thorough analysis of the current knowledge of psychotropic medications both in the field of biomedical research and in the human and social sciences."

GAM also "recognize(s) the symbolic aspects of medication and require(s) recognition of its multiple, and at times contradictory, meanings in the lives of users and various individuals involved in psychiatric treatment."

Now I have no idea what this means, particularly the symbolism medication may have. If you have a headache, you take an analgesic. Is that symbolic?

The only paper that I could find on Pub Med or on the internet is the one that I quoted from above. It is claimed that this strategy qualifies as best practices in Quebec but the reference link is dead. Many of the references are not there. They did mention research with 26 people with serious mental illnesses and provided a table to demonstrate the results of their research. That table shows that there was a decline in the number of medications taken at the end of the program. Is that good or bad? No idea. They may think so.

If you have a serious mental illness, your doctor will prescribe medication. That doctor is usually a psychiatrist who has six years of medical school, one year of internship, and five years of residency training to qualify as a psychiatrist. He or she should be well aware of what to expect from what is prescribed and should discuss the effects of that medication on you including side effects. The prescription will be dispensed by a licensed pharmacist with five years of university training who will pick up any drug-drug interactions that the doc may have missed.

Both the doctor and the pharmacist have ethical obligations and responsibilities to you as well as legal responsibilities dictated by their regulatory colleges. Your buddy, the peer, has none of the above education, ethical or legal responsibilities. They might say by way of support, "that sounds like a side effect. I had something similar but it went away in a few days. If it doesn't, better see the doctor or talk to your pharmacist". Perfectly legitimate. But you really should not be talking to him about the legitimacy of the prescription or whether you should even take it. To be perfectly pragmatic, you can sue your doc for malpractice and/or report him to his regulatory body, but what of your lay peer?

If you had diabetes, would you learn from a peer how to manage it or would you work with your endocrinologist, dietician and other regulated health professionals?

Why, when it comes to mental illness, is it considered alright to get your pharmaceutical and treatment advice from a lay person?

Planning Mental Health Services Rationally

By Dr David Laing Dawson

Over the years I have been several times involved in planning mental health services, sometimes in a general and wide sense, sometimes specific programs. In each case I usually ask, "How much money do we have to spend? What is the budget?" And usually there is no answer to this question. The game is not played that way. First the proposal to compete with other proposals and then, within a highly politicized process, the allocation of funds.

This means of course, that the words are being sold, promoted. Not the actual evidence based possibility of major effectiveness with consideration of budget. But rather the most pleasing, hopeful, expansive words of promise (with fewest political complications) are being sold and often funded. This may be a good way to fund an arts program, but for health, we really should turn to science.

If we say, instead, "We have 10 million dollars to spend to prevent suicide in a particular state or province; how should we spend it for best results?" then our thinking might be clarified for us. What do we actually know about suicide and suicide prevention? What do studies from various parts of the world show? Where are the high risk populations? Which ones can we actually target?

Then we might look at the large range of social and economic factors that comprise risk factors that indirectly, or at a distance, contribute to a high suicide rate, and pass on these. They are usually broad conditions that can be gradually improved, and should be gradually improved through political action and do require political will and good economic times. (housing, minimum wage, employment, social programs, education)

Then we could look at specific high-risk populations and figure how we could spend that 10 million effectively to measurably reduce the suicide rate.

Then we might notice that a **very high risk group for completed**

suicide comprises people too-late identified as suffering from severe mental illness, recently discharged psychiatric patients, and especially those suffering from a severe and chronic mental illness who drop out of treatment and/or stop their medications.

And then we can ask if there is a way of spending that 10 million dollars to improve and repair the services offered this group of people. They are identifiable. They are at high risk. And it is possible with limited money to enhance the programs that serve them. Especially during visits to emergency, drop-in clinics, and family doctors, and then in the years following diagnosis and/or discharge from hospital.

Of course we need to improve the resilience and mental health of our children, if we can. But not as a means to reduce the suicide rate, but rather for overall success of our children as adults. And this means, not a suicide prevention program, but rather more money and support for the educational system and improvements in this system utilizing all we know about learning, nutrition, physical health, exercise, social growth, stress management, disability accommodation, **ensuring each child has some success and a chance to belong**.

When it comes to suicide then, we don't need a "national strategy". We need to continue to improve all our services and our lives, with improvements in our educational systems, income support and equality, a healthy economy and good jobs, improved general health care systems and easy access to same, addictions programs, income and social support for the elderly, affordable housing...... And we need to turn our attention to those people we know to be at especially high risk for suicide (sufferers of severe mental illness, recently discharged patients) and improve our services and access to services for these people.

Families, Privacy and Hospital Suicides

By Marvin Ross

One of the constant themes in my writing of mental illness is the need to involve the family. And so, when I read a lengthy account of the suicide of a young 20 year old girl that appeared in my local paper, what jumped out at me was that she had requested that her family not be involved with her illness or treatment. She wanted to spare the family grief and, it seems that the doctors went along with her.

The young girl had a number of suicide attempts while in hospital and the family was told none of it. Dr Peter Cook, one of the psychiatrists, told the newspaper that "We were obligated to protect the privacy of Nicole. She was an adult." The other shrink said that confidentiality between patient and doctor is "sacrosanct." Nicole did not want to share her medical information with her family.

Sadly, this young lady is not the only suicide in the past little while at this hospital. There have been 9 – 3 in hospital, 2 of patients on leave and 4 outpatients. To its credit, the hospital did commission an external review to see if things could be improved. One of the recommendations was for "closer collaboration with families."

Now, maybe the outcome would not have been different if the family was involved but we don't know that. And, the privacy legislation is pretty confining but there are ways to get around them if the medical staff really care. The hospital recently established a family resource centre as the result of a donation from a philanthropist friend of mine. It was difficult to get them to accept the gift but they did and it is being used and it is being well publicized to families.

At the time we were negotiating for a family resource centre at the hospital, I wrote an op ed for the local paper on the need that families have for inclusion with staff when their loved ones are being treated. Aside from pointing out the anger that families have towards being ignored, I mentioned the very sensible guidelines that were produced by the Mental Health Commission of Canada for family caregiver inclusion. And I mentioned this:

"Very few, if any, mental health facilities have adopted these recommendations despite the fact that about 70 per cent of those with serious mental illness live with their families according to the Mood Disorders study. And family caregivers spend 27 hours a week caring for their ill relative according to the EUFAMI survey. That is five hours longer than the average in other countries surveyed by EUFAMI."

I don't know if St Joes ever did adopt these recommendations and I do know that the Privacy Act is very restrictive. But, with a little effort, it can be sidestepped as I pointed out in a Huffington Post Blog.

I was basing what I had to say on an excellent paper on the topic that had recently been published by Dr. Richard O'Reilly, a professor of psychiatry, Dr. John Gray, an adjunct professor of psychiatry along with J. Jung, a student in the Faculty of Health Science at Western University.

I said this in my post:

They point out that clinicians often don't even bother to ask their patients if they have permission to involve family.

If they do and the patient refuses, then they should take the time to explore the reasons for this refusal. Many patients don't understand why it is important and do agree to allow their families information once it is explained to them. In some cases, there is some information they do not want shared (like sexual activity and/or drug use) and the staff can ensure that this information is not shared. Staff can also inform families of pertinent facts in meetings with the patient present. This often allays patient fears and is similar to the approach recommended in the UK and by the Mental Health Commission of Canada.

In those cases where no consent is given, the staff can give general information to the families and receive vital information from the family. The family can tell the doctors about new emerging symptoms, worsening of symptoms and medication side effects, all of which should be crucial information.

Until such time as political jurisdictions reform the privacy legislation, mental health staff can do far more to open the channels of communication with families for the betterment of their patients. It is time they do so.

I was pleasantly surprised that at a meeting with St Joes staff just after this was published, one of them told me that this blog was being read by staff and was being circulated within the hospital.

It seems that not sufficient attention may have been paid to that. I hope that more attention is paid to involving families so that these tragic events can be minimized going forward.

More on Families, Privacy And Suicide

By Dr David Laing Dawson

Much of psychiatry is about **convincing** people to do things that will improve their mood, their health, and their lives. Exercise, better diet, overcoming fears, taking necessary medication, stop taking harmful substances, go to bed earlier, turn off electronics, find balance in your life, join something to overcome loneliness, stop procrastinating, call a relative, tell your husband, plan your day, stop worrying about things you cannot control, take baby steps, take medication regularly as prescribed, go for blood tests, enjoy small pleasures, scream at someone rather than cut yourself....

It is not in the DSM V (I think) but we know "no man is an island". We are social beings. Maybe not to the extent of bees and ants, but no less than chimpanzees. **We are never fully independent life forms**. Even a hermit has a relationship (albeit a distorted and contrary one) with the community and family he or she is rejecting.

We also know that the quick impulse to say to the doctor, "Don't tell my family." or "I don't want my family involved." is often derived from shame, guilt, a sense of failure, and sometimes the opposite, a genuine wish to not burden the other. This is further complicated in the teen and youth years by an ongoing negotiation with respect to power, control, individuation, responsibility. We also know in these years the adolescent often says, in the same breath, "I hate you. Give me a hug." "Get out of my life. Drive me to the mall." "Don't tell my dad. Please tell my dad so he can protect me."

And we also know that persons suffering from severe anxiety and depression develop a sort of tunnel vision that excludes broad levels of social awareness and understanding. "Leave me alone." And people suffering from a psychotic illness often harbour delusions about family members. "She's controlling me."

So, absolutely, when the young person says, "Don't involve my family." professionals should explore this, and then convince the patient otherwise unless there is **good evidence** that keeping the family (parents, sibs) away will be ultimately better for this patient.

Cockamamie Views From Anti-Psychiatric Advocate

By Marvin Ross

Bonnie Burstow, the anti-psychiatry scholarship donor at the University of Toronto, gave a lecture in December on her book called *Psychiatry and the Business of Madness*. The lecture is on youtube for those of you who have the stomach to watch it. I managed 38 minutes of the hour talk and it is so full of absurdities that, frankly, it defies reality.

I recently wrote about her scholarship on the Huffington Post and that was followed by a number of other critiques of that endeavour – none favourable. To m Blackwell, the National Post medical writer, called it an affront to science that could do harm. "This is a case where academic freedom should be quashed," Edward Shorter, a U of T professor and expert in the history of psychiatry, told Blackwell. Dr. Joel Paris, a McGill University psychiatrist, is quoted saying he is ashamed of the University.

I can only imagine what they would have said if they saw this lecture so allow me to summarize the first half and point out the errors.

Bonnie begins by saying that psychiatry is so inherently wrong that it just cannot continue. She points out that psychiatrists are so powerful that they are the only ones in society who have the right to take away someone's freedom. They have king like power like those of the 16th and 17th centuries who had the power to exile citizens forever.

Now she says these views are based on thousands of interviews and attending 15 consent and capacity board hearings. If she really did attend those meetings, she could not believe what she said and by equating shrinks to autocratic monarchs, she suggests that there is no recourse to anything they do. Each jurisdiction allows for holding someone for observation and the rules differ but are all basically the same. For the purpose of this blog, I will comment on Ontario since

Bonnie lives in Ontario as do I.

To begin with, psychiatrists are not the only ones to have the power to put someone in the hospital for observation. Any MD can do that based on very specific criteria. It is not arbitrary. The initial period is for 72 hours only after which the person is to be discharged, or can agree to remain voluntarily. If they still pose a threat to themselves or others, they can be held for a further 2 week period but that cannot be ordered by the doctor who originally signed the 72 hour committal. A second doctor must agree that it is necessary and sign the forms.

The patient is then told by the patient rights advocate that they can appeal if they do not agree and they will be supplied with a legal aid lawyer. This results in a capacity hearing before a board 15 of which Bonnie attended.

This is hardly imprisoning anyone nor is it done without respect for individual rights. Bonnie describes this as bringing the weight of the entire state, police, hospitals, families, universities who have been all sucked into this system. At the very centre of this conspiracy are the big pharma companies.

To illustrate what she calls the lack of substance to psychiatry, she recounts the experiences of her friend, Amy. For about 30 years, Amy has periodically taken off all her clothes and run down the street pounding on doors yelling "emergency, emergency". Concerned homeowners call the cops who come and take her to hospital where she is locked up for a period of time. This has happened in various jurisdictions all over North America and Bonnie feels it is ridiculous. Her activities are simply "outside our comfort zone" so we define her as dangerous and sick. Bonnie does not even think people should call the cops.

I don't know about you but if this happened in my neighbourhood, I'd call 9-1-1. I'm not sure what I would think but escaping a rapist would come to mind, or an abusive spouse or having been held against her will would be at the top of my thinking. The police are best able to deal with that. If they can find no reasonable reason for this behaviour, then of course they would take her to the emergency room.

This example led her to talk about violence of the mentally ill and a long discussion on the impossibility of psychiatrists being able to predict who may or may not become violent. She is correct on that score but her argument that is often heard about those with mental illness never being violent is absurd. Those who are untreated and those who are untreated and substance abusers are at far greater risk of violence than others. This link from the Treatment Advocacy Centre lists all the studies that demonstrate this fact.

She then goes on to talk about how mass shootings involve people who are often on psych meds and that it is the meds that likely cause these shootings. Psychiatrist Joe Pierre writing in Psychology Today argues that "In the vast majority of cases, we don't have access to their medical records and we certainly don't know if the medications, even if prescribed or otherwise obtained, were actually being taken."

"And then, of course, there's the issue of correlation vs. causality. After all, I'm fairly certain all known mass murderers were drinkers of tap water, which has also been linked to violent outbursts."

At this point, Professor Burstow switches into "refuting" the concept of mental illness. She states that only a body can have an illness. A mind cannot be ill as it is only used for thinking. I kid you not! That is what she said.

She then goes on to say that the hallmarks of paranoid schizophrenia are paranoia and delusions of grandeur. What happens to the paranoia and the grandeur when the person dies and there is just a corpse. She asks her audience if any of them have ever seen a corpse with delusions and, since no one has, schizophrenia fails the test of an illness.

What can anyone say when confronted with this? Professor Burstow has failed the test of physiology. The brain is an organ that allows us the ability to think, speak, make decisions, and so on. Does she have any idea how it is that we can think in the first place? Obviously not. This summary provides an overview of the differences in the brains of those with schizophrenia compared to normal brains. There are numerous differences.

And this is a study showing the abnormalities in the brain of autopsied people with schizophrenia. Which of these abnormalities results in paranoia and delusions of grandeur is not known but the brains are different.

I gave up when she began talking about the longitudinal studies by Harrow in Chicago. This researcher followed a group of people with schizophrenia for 20 years and checked on them every five. What he found was that some people were able to go off meds and do well and they were doing better than those on meds. I've written about this a number of times and, in one of my Huffington Post blogs, I had this to say:

79 per cent and 64 per cent of the patients were on medication at 10- and 15-year follow ups. Those who were not on medication, did better on the outcome measures than those who were on but would that not be expected? Why they stopped the medication or were removed from it by their doctors was not explained, but we can presume that it was because they did not need the medication. In fact, Harrow states that not all schizophrenia patients are alike and that one treatment fits all is "not consonant with the current data or with clinical experience." His data suggests that there are unique differences in those who can go off medications compared to those who cannot. In a paper Harrow just published in March, he points out that it is not possible to predict who may be able to go off medication and those who need the long term treatment. Intensified research is needed.

It just isn't that simple, Bonnie. She did go on but I could not take anymore so ended there.

Understanding the Disease Model

By Dr David Laing Dawson

I had a friendly argument with a colleague the other day. He reminded me that we had been arguing about this topic for 40 years. I think our arguments are mostly ways of clarifying our own thoughts about a very complicated question involving concepts of mind, of cognition, and of the brain, that organ who's function makes us human.

Mental illness, disease, disorder, serious mental illness, continuum, spectrum, problem, affliction – when is it both valid and useful to consider aberrations (or non-typical) variations in behaviour and thought, illnesses? In some ways these words are just words, and few would care if we referred to arthritis in any of these terms. But when it comes to behavior, thought, and communication (rather than joint flexibility and joint pain) our dearly held beliefs about self, autonomy, will, power, consciousness, and mortality come into play. The discussion becomes political.

Before the medical disease concept evolved in the 18th and 19th century most afflictions were considered very personal and specific, and the causes very personal and specific. An obvious grouping of afflictions might mean God was particularly disappointed in a whole family or tribe. The Miasmists thought that perhaps God did not have that much control over everything and proposed that the causes might be found in the atmosphere, the miasma, physical, spiritual, emotional. An excess or a deficit. The Naturopaths liked this idea but knowing nothing of physiology, metabolism, or nutrition, concocted potions and powders with dozens of ingredients positing that the body might choose from the lot that which it needed. Each of these ideas continues to echo in the pursuit of health today. Especially in the commercial exploitation of our pursuit of health.

The disease model is founded on the idea that if a number of people suffer the same symptoms and signs, and if their affliction follows the same course with the same outcome then perhaps these people suffer from the same "thing". This in turn raises the possibility that the cause is the same in all cases and that a treatment that works for one will work for the others. To study this we need to name (diagnose) the thing and describe it's symptoms, signs, and natural course. Given that we are biological beings it is reasonable to think that some of the signs of these diseases will be biological, and that the causes might be as well. But first the chore is to observe, study, collate, find groupings and test this hypothesis.

In a sense the disease model has picked off all the low hanging fruit, those illnesses with very specific causes and courses and, of course, those for which we have found specific treatments, cures and prevention.

The disease model, and some rudimentary epidemiology, led Dr. John Snow to the source of an outbreak of cholera and then to speculate that the cause, residing in the water supply, "behaved as if it were a living organism". This before we knew about bacteria, let alone viruses, prions, DNA, and neurohomones.

The same disease model has led to the near eradication of Polio. Drs. Alzheimer and Kraeplin applied the disease model to older people with failing cognitive processes and singled out an illness we now call Alzheimers. Dr. Alzheimer had the advantage of being able to examine the brains of his patients soon after diagnosis. Dr. Kraeplin went on to apply the disease model to a younger group of patients with peculiar cognitive difficulties, some similar to dementia, some not, and singled out a group he called dementia praecox, and another group he called manic depressive. Similarly and more recently the disease model singled out autism from the broader group of mentally handicapped children.

The disease model also allows us to study afflictions and find remedies before, sometimes long before we establish with certainty the causes of the affliction. Who on earth but a cruel idealogue would want us to stop treating and reducing suffering until we find an exact and specific cause of the affliction in question, be it cancer, arthritis, or schizophrenia. Yet that is the cant of the anti-psychiatry folks.

Yet the disease model allows us, sometimes by accident, to find remedies that work, can be proven to work, before we nail down etiology. Now, as mentioned earlier, the disease model has picked off the low hanging fruit, those afflictions caused by single alien organisms, and very specific genetic aberrations. We are left with those that are undoubtedly the product of complex combinations of genetic vulnerability, epigenetic influences in the womb, environmental influences, developmental timing, excesses, and deficits.

But we should no more give up on the disease model for schizophrenia and depression than for heart disease, cancer, arthritis, ALS, and dementia.

Our argument was actually about OCD. Having some Obsessive and Compulsive traits can be an asset of course, and of great help in medical school, while extreme OC traits can be debilitating. The "D" of OCD is the initial for "disorder" of course, but is OCD, in annoying to debilitating form, a disease?

Unfortunately the word "disease" has become freighted with negative association, and for my friend, too much associated with "biological cause".

Ultimately he may think of OCD as a mind problem, while I may think of it as a mind/brain problem, but it is the discipline of the medical disease concept that allows us to study **it** and find remedies we can test.

About the Authors

David Laing Dawson

David Laing Dawson is a psychiatrist and former chief of psychiatry at the Hamilton Psychiatric Hospital (now part of St Joseph's Health Care) and associate professor of psychiatry at McMaster University Faculty of Health Sciences also in Hamilton Ontario.

His academic books are S*chizophrenia in Focus with* *H. Munroe-Blum, and G. Bartolucci, Human Sciences: Press, New York, N.Y., 1983*

and *Relationship Management: Treatment of the Borderline Patient* – with *Harriet MacMillan*: *Brunner/Mazel, New York, 1993*

David is also a story teller with a number of published mysteries such as:

Last Rights (novel) –St. Martin's Press, New York, N.Y. Macmillan of Canada, Toronto, 1990 Published in Europe by; Klim, Denmark; Frjals Fjolmidlun HF, Iceland; Rowohlt, Germany; Bzztoh, Holland; Chivers Press, England; Forlag, Sweden; Edit Du Seuil, Paris, France.

Double Blind (novel) – St. Martin's Press, New York, N.Y. Macmillan of Canada, Toronto, 1992. Published in Europe by; Klim, Denmark; Frjals Fjolmidlun HF, Iceland; Rowohlt, Germany ; Bzztoh, Holland; Chivers Press, England; Forlag, Sweden; Edit Du Seuil, Paris, France Available on Amazon.com

Essondale (novel) –Macmillan of Canada, Toronto, 1993 re-issued by Bridgeross Communications, 2010 3, released as paperback by Bridgeross Communications 2008 A psychological thriller.

The Intern (novel) – Macmillan of Canada, Toronto, 1996 re-issued by Bridgeross Communications 2011

Slide in All Direction (novel) – Bridgeross Communications 2008

Don't Look Down (novel) – Bridgeross Communications, 2009

He is also the author of the self help book The Adolescent

Owner's Manual – Published by Bridgeross Communications, 2010

If that wasn't enough, Dawson is also a noted play write and film maker both documentary and feature as well as being an artist and co-owner of the Gallery on the Bay in Hamilton Ontario.

He still finds time to treat patients.

Marvin Ross

Marvin Ross, had been writing books, newspaper, magazine articles and teaching business communications since the late 1970's. His first book was *"Economics, Opportunity and Crime"* but he quickly switched to humour with *"Cover Your Ass or How To Survive in A Government Bureaucracy"* using the pseudonym Bureaucrat X. David Shaw illustrated what became a very popular book in Canada.

He and Shaw went on to do *"Daddy Dearest: A Guide for First Time Fathers"*; *"Sorry Daddy: A First time Father's Guide"* and *"Reigning Cats and Dogs: A Lighthearted Look at Pets and Their Owners"*.

Ross then switched to more serious topics with books on Alzheimer's, eyes and other medical and health writing for a variety of papers and eventually websites. He has covered many medical conferences to report on new advances in cardiology, cancer, digestive diseases, respiration and neurology and psychiatry. His specialized services have been used to develop continuing medical education programs for physicians and to write summarizes of medical meetings.

In 2008, he decided to publish his own book on *Schizophrenia* which had the subtitle *Medicine's Mystery - Society's Shame*. That book has received considerable praise in both North America and Europe and Ross found himself quickly learning about the publishing industry. As a result, Bridgeross switched its focus from writing to publishing.

Bridgeross quickly developed interest from authors wishing to write about serious mental illness many of whom have submitted proposals. To date, Bridgeross has accepted and published a number of highly recommended titles in that subject matter - one by a mother discussing her fight to help her daughter; three by people with schizophrenia (an artist, a psychologist and a neuroscientist), one by a mother with schizophrenia co-written with her daughter and a memoir on a family of 10 working together to help a sibling with schizophrenia who died of lung cancer.

Three of the Bridgeross books have been listed as among the top books on schizophrenia by US psychiatrist, E Fuller Torrey, in his latest edition of the classic *Understanding Schizophrenia A Manual For Families*. The three titles are *Schizophrenia Medicine's Mystery Society's Shame* by Bridgeross publisher, Marvin Ross, *After Her Brain Broke: Helping My Daughter Recover Her Sanity* by Susan Inman, and Dr. Carolyn Dobbins' *What A Life Can Be: One Therapist's Take on Schizoaffective Disorder.*

Mr Ross, the publisher, Torrey describes as "one of the leading Canadian advocates for individuals with serious psychiatric disorders." Previously, healthyplace.com, an award winning metal health website based in San Antonio, listed 2 of the above 3 books as must haves for people with serious mental illnesses. Two of them are *After Her Brain Broke* and *What A Life Can Be*. The other is *My Schizophrenic Life: The Road to Recovery From Mental Illness* by Sandra Yuen MacKay. Sandra was named the Courage to Come Back winner in mental health in BC in 2012 and was one of the five Faces of Mental Illness in Canada.

As a family member with a son with schizophrenia, Mr Ross has been blogging for a number of years on mental illness issues for the Huffington Post as well as Mind You.

CPSIA information can be obtained
at www.ICGtesting.com
Printed in the USA
BVHW082024040219
539409BV00002B/272/P